Nobody Rides for Free

Nobody Rides for Free: A Drifter in the Americas is a classic picaresque tale in the tradition of Don Quixote and Jack Kerouac – a luckless guy in search of himself in all the wrong places, fueled by way too much booze and the ghost of a drunken father stalking him every inch of the way. Hughes reports unflinchingly his failures and bad decisions: his striking out with girls; his health issues; and, botched attempts at teaching English. The suspense is brutal. Will the next ride be the one with the serial killer, or will he find the woman of his dreams?

– ROBERTA RICH, author of *The Midwife of Venice*

Nobody Rides for Free: A Drifter in the Americas is quite simply one of the best travel memoirs I've ever read, an exhilarating ride from start to finish. A drifter with the soul of a poet and the liver of a drunk, Hughes' encounters with Florida psychopaths, monkey attacks in Ecuador and swimming in the piranha-infested Amazon, are like sitting down for beers with your favourite old friend who's been gone too long. A punk rock travelogue of the highest calibre, by turns moving, hilarious, and horrific, this is an awe-inspiring tale of a journey undertaken by very few, and survived by even fewer.

– TERESA MCWHIRTER, author of *Dirtbags*

In *Nobody Rides for Free*, John Hughes takes a bizarre journey through Latin America and beyond, with misadventures that will leave you both hysterical and horrified. With an amazing ability to shimmy out of trouble whether from a sex-crazed truck driver or a mutant woman hell-bent on getting married, Hughes' narrow escapes on the road will have you shaking your head at the craziness of it all. As I turned the pages I began to beg him to stop hitchhiking; of course he never did, yet somehow, somehow survived! John Hughes is a true road warrior.

– NATASHA STANISZEWSKI, TSN sports anchor

Thumbing a ride with John Hughes is as exhilarating, terrifying, gratifying and humbling as the real thing. Travelling his pages takes the reader *WAY* off the beaten path: Blasting through barricades of the intellect; careening over philosophical potholes; fixing a flat tire of memory; and grabbing that downhill fix of pure joy. This is one ride you don't want to pass up.

    – CAROLINA DE RYK, Host, CBC Radio, Daybreak North

Nobody Rides For Free: A Drifter in the Americas is a reader's delight. The pages are filled with adventure, laced with true grit, descriptive flare and dipped in palatable wordsmith purity. I chewed through the book anxiously, being pulled, page-by-page, from roadside stops, over state lines and across countries. John Hughes' vivid descriptions broadened my travel experiences without even having to leave my living room. This book has the power to inspire readers to kick life into another gear, buy a plane ticket and live a little more.

    – KELLAND SUNDAHL, CTV

You know that trip you always thought you'd take? The one where you were going to travel the world on a bicycle using only your wits and what you could carry in a backpack to get you through? The one where you would wake up after nights of drinking with strangers and beautiful women, in a place where it was always warm, a place where the alcohol was always flowing – and other party favours were also readily available. Well, John Hughes has not only done what we've only dreamt of, but he survived it! Luckily John has more wit than the average person or he might not have lived to tell this tale. *Nobody Rides for Free* is an entertaining and insightful story about a trip I am now very, very glad I never got around to taking myself.

    – DAN REYNISH, CBC Radio One

Nobody Rides for Free:
A Drifter in the Americas

John Francis Hughes

BookThug

Maps copyright © Jesse Huisken, 2012
Copy edited by Ruth Zuchter

The production of this book was made possible through the generous assistance
of the Ontario Arts Council and the Canada Council for the Arts.

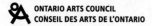

Also issued as: ISBN 978-1-927040-15-7 (epub)

LIBRARY AND ARCHIVES CANADA CATALOGUING IN PUBLICATION

Hughes, John Francis
    Nobody rides for free : a drifter in the Americas/ John Francis Hughes.

ISBN 978-1-927040-04-1

1. Hughes, John Francis – Travel. 2. Latin America – Description and travel.
3. North America – Description and travel. 4. Bicycle touring – Latin America.
5. Bicycle touring – North America. I. Title.

F1409.3.H85 2012   918.04'39   C2012-900601-7

CONTENTS

When I first met John Hughes, I thought to myself: "Is that guy all right in the head?" But what was I to expect? After all, orgies for Yogi Bear fetishists do tend to attract a unique breed. It took me 45 minutes and having to endure several awkward "Hey there Boo Boo's" to figure out this was, in fact, the wrong John Hughes. John Hughes is a fairly common name after all. Hopefully he'll trot out a classy pen name now that he is a published author. You know something like Dandy Nib Quillson.

Still. The proper, first time I met John Francis Hughes, I have to be honest, I still thought: "Is that guy all right in the head? I mean, did something happen to him?" Over the course of the next two years – in which John and I developed an intense friendship, definitely a partnership, certainly, a spiritual kinship, and without a doubt a brotherly bond – I would get my answers.

John and I were brought together by the taxpayers of Canada in somewhat of an odd social experiment. John was a city boy: a former hard-core bike courier from the mean yet progressive streets of Vancouver. I too was from a concrete jungle in my own monkey suit. I worked as a mental health councillor with the dregs of Toronto found lurking in the urban shadows – be they homeless, federal criminals or straight up crazies.

Both John and I had enjoyed our separate lives but wanted something more, something with a bit of cache. So we both went to journalism school, then got jobs with the Canadian Broadcasting Corporation. We were then promptly sent from our separate civilized metropolitan existences and banished to the rural backwoods in the middle of the country. Indeed, we were right in the middle of Canada's most seemingly unremarkable province. John and I now comprised the two-man journalist crew for CBC in Prince Albert, Saskatchewan. John in radio and me in TV.

I believe Charlie Dickens said it best: It was the best of times; it was the worst of times. Looking back on it now though, as long as John was around, the pendulum always swung its way to the best of times.

John Hughes strikes an imposing figure. There is an intensity about him. His second skin – a heavily buckled leather jacket – shouts out the chorus to his anthem and personal philosophy so he doesn't have to: Accept's *Balls to the Wall*. Oh yeah…! His head has dabbled in its fair share of banging. He's 6'1" and 220 of all muscle. Although I am surely painting a picture of John as a hired goon, his greatest weapon is his brain. John is one of the most educated, well-read and introspective persons I know. He is a dedicated practitioner of transcendental meditation. This guy is so thoughtful he should be a tenured Ivy League professor. When I first went to his house, it was stocked with books as if he already was: *For Whom the Bell Tolls; Crime and Punishment; Decline and Fall of the Roman Empire* and the *Bhagavad Gita* to name just a tiny few. So in love with books was John, he refused to cheat on them with a television. His affections for the printed word inspired him to tell me early in our friendship he was going to write a book of his own. I know, I know, we all have met those people who make such ridiculously pompous declarations but hey, they're just assholes. John is different. I knew then, it was just a matter of time before my fingers flipped through his pages. When I asked him what it would be about, he told me he has had some pretty wild adventures in his life thus far he could write about.

x

Believe me; John has had some novel-worthy *adventures* in his life as you will find out for yourself as you devour *Nobody Rides For Free*. I've been fortunate to ride shotgun for some of them that did not make it into the book.

As part of our job with the CBC, John and I had to travel the back roads of Saskatchewan for our news stories. Sometimes these trips would last up to eight hours with only the sound of unearthly huge bugs thunking against our windshield to entertain us. We had to talk for the sake of keeping our sanity. And we did – every second of the journey. These talks were and remain my most cherished memories from my time with John. He's a very honest guy. And John does not have a problem sharing stories from some of the darker chapters of his life. I mean we all have baggage but in John's case, it would be best to hire some help if he was going to the airport, is all I'm saying. The more he disclosed it was like another bizarre layer of decay coming away from his slightly rotting onion. And I was like a hyped-up freshmen forensic student at his first day at the cadaver farm: so disturbing, so fascinating, and yet so wonderful to learn about my new best friend.

I remember one particular sordid tale of decomposition he told me. John admitted over lunch that he once worked cleaning homes but with this caveat: he did it in the buff – as was the client's request. What do you say to that? "Yeah I know what you mean." just doesn't cut it.

Long before Sarah Palin ever had the idea to go rogue or even learned how to spell it and properly pronounce it, John Hughes had been the poster boy for the "going rogue lifestyle". He has a sense of fearlessness that has opened a lot of doors to new and crazy experiences. But in doing so, he left himself exposed to getting hit on the ass on the back swing by these doors as they wildly swung open.

One of our CBC assignments involved heading many, many hours north in the dead of winter to cover a rough and tumble Aboriginal hockey tournament. So north I believe we spotted the Abominable

Snowman and Sasquatch trying to sell home-made lemonade slushies at a road-side table. Our destination was a First Nations community called La Loche. It had a reputation any straight-up; bad-ass gangster would be envious of. This town was rough. We rolled in in a marked CBC vehicle and all heads turned and eyes narrowed. We were marked men. These people had not forgotten how their ancestors were screwed out of their land and now were looking to settle the score with anyone a closer shade to the snow then they were. If that welcome wasn't bad enough we received a greeting most foul upon entering our lodging.

John gasped: "Oh gawd it smells like poo on a heat source!"

I, in my best Doctor Watson, retorted: "Well here's your problem." As I pointed to what was in fact some sort of fecal matter on the radiator.

Like I said, this town was rough. But as was our custom John and I left the "motel" and went exploring – hoping on some level while we were out some sort of nonexistent maid service would come and miraculously appear taking care of the literal hot mess we were trying to escape from. We decided to take the vehicle down a snow mobile trail in order to get a nice shot of the sunset on the frozen lake. John was at the wheel (a dangerous scenario as you will soon read about) and it wasn't long before the truck was hubcap deep in snow. John always the active problem solver – gassed it. Suddenly we found ourselves door handle deep – stranded in the middle of absolutely nowhere, with no one in sight and our sight quickly fading as the winter night enveloped us.

It is a proven, scientific fact that John Hughes and these types of situations have some sort of magnetism for one another.

But as with many of the tales in John's book, just as it appeared all hope was lost – a way out. A bunch of snowmobilers came upon us. They ridiculed us in a way that made Abu Ghraib seem like a Sandals resort until they finally and mercifully decided to break out their shovels and dig us out.

xii

As the men worked and our vehicle's tires reappeared like four black round Lazarus from their snowy tomb, things were looking up. Then just as we were about pull off the snowmobile trail and get back to whatever this Northern Saskatchewan adventure dared to give us… *the catch.*

One of the men asked for some money.

It is a lesson John has repeatedly and painfully had to learn. In many an uncomfortable, humiliating, tragic, comedic, downright-dangerous, intense and surreal situation: *Nobody Rides for Free.*

I asked a question at the beginning of my friendship with John: "Is this guy all right in the head?" I did find out. And you too, dear reader, will be able to come to you own conclusions. All you have to do is keep reading. John Francis Hughes has laid bare his odyssey thoughtfully and beautifully in these pages. It is a narrative sojourn which engages and challenges, while opening an aperture to the arcane world of 1990s road culture. It reveals insights into the human condition about why we need to keep moving, how we navigate our way there and once *there,* asks the question: Have we ultimately arrived or are we just at a crossroads, duty-bound to saddle up for the next journey?

All passages have a price because *Nobody Rides for Free.* Enjoy.

CHRIS KAYANIOTES
September 2011

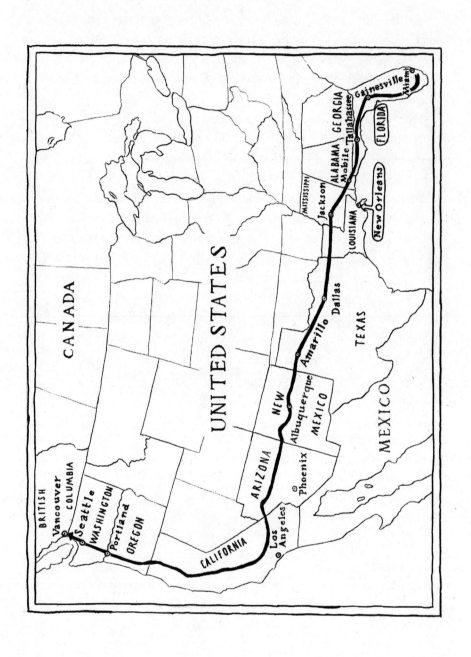

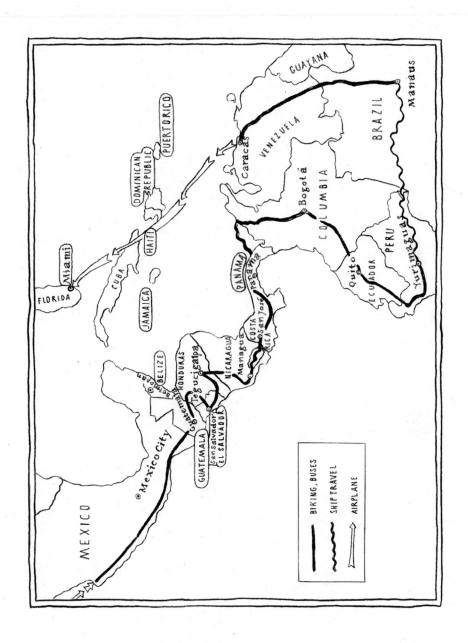

BIKING, BUSES

SHIP TRAVEL

AIRPLANE

An open road, where I can breathe,
where the lowest low is calling to me. – BECK

It was January 1996 and government deputies had assigned me a seat in the Immigration Office at Miami International Airport. They held me up for my ragged Mayan clothing, matted long hair and muck-stained running shoes. I had 75 dollars in my pocket, carried no ticket home and planned to cut through the US after six months of free-wheeling in Central and South America. One guy in particular wanted to know what I had been doing down there. Had I brought any drugs back with me? Any political involvement in Peru or Colombia? Did I really think I could make it to Vancouver on 75 bucks?

I'd come to an understanding with a Peruvian army officer weeks before on the subjects of politics and drugs, and had nothing more to say about either one. I wanted to talk about getting home. It wouldn't take me long to hitchhike. There was even a bed for me once I got to Los Angeles, or so I thought. A big country lay between Miami and Vancouver, but I swore I'd make short work of it. The immigration guy shot me a disgusted look, shaking his head and griping, "Seventy-five bucks? Gimme a break."

The official wore charcoal-grey trousers, an over-starched button-down shirt and gleaming gold insignia. A coiffed moustache added pompous flair, and his smugness showed how pleased he was that the uniform impressed me. But it wasn't the regalia that turned my head, it was all that starch. I thought, damn, this guy looks like he'd snap in two if he bent over to tie his shoelaces. He could probably use a drink. I know I could. That would have been just the thing. I'd spent my time in South America riding a bicycle through mishaps and bad luck. Liquor was my exit from reality. At 35 cents for a bottle of beer and 50 for a shot of rum, it was a bargain I couldn't refuse.

But booze would have to wait. Even though a relative calm prevailed among airport security paranoiacs back in 1996, I could tell the well-starched dude was leaning toward not letting me into the country. Despite passing through the metal detector and not rousing the drug-sniffing dogs, I couldn't have been one of his all-star prospects for the day. The stench of cheap alcohol percolated from every pore. I wasn't drunk, understand, but I had been recently. My liquor-addled brain was trying to figure out if he'd send me back to Venezuela or deport me to Canada.

Either prospect was disconcerting. If he rerouted me to Venezuela, I was well and truly screwed. It had cost me 100 dollars to fly from Caracas to Miami. I knew that a handful of gringos had hopped freighters from Venezuela to Houston. But if I did that, I'd still have to shell out to cross the Caribbean and the Gulf of Mexico, only to sail into more red tape at the docks in Texas. Deportation to Canada would have been an improvement, but probably still dire. It was mid-winter, with the average temperature there about -25. My final stop was Vancouver where it's warm, but I figured on long odds that the security guy would hook me up with a ticket to the West Coast, and better ones, he'd send me to Ottawa or Montreal. That would strand me thousands of frozen miles from home. What I hoped to do was hitch north through Florida, veer west at the panhandle, and move on through the South until I reached California. From there I'd head north again until I hit Vancouver.

Starch-man had fun detaining me, popping his head in the doorway every 15 minutes to smirk. I sat, stinking, waiting for the verdict. Hours later, he marched me to another room. I don't recall the title etched on the nameplate, but it gave an ominous sense of moving up the hierarchy. Starch-man snorted and left. My fate hung in the balance for 20 more minutes. The door swung open on well-oiled hinges, when a slight, white-haired man in rumpled Immigration Department clothing entered the room. He told me to hand over my passport, stamped it with a six-month visa and wished me a pleasant stay. I was dumbstruck. A visa? Who, in 1996, had heard of a Canadian needing a visa to travel in the United States? Not me, that much was sure. But the paperwork didn't matter; I was in.

Travelling to Vancouver from Miami on 75 bucks would make for a thorny slog, but I was game. Fired with a new sense of adventure, I walked out of the airport, anticipating the highway. The first new thing was the chill. A colder wind than the ones in Caracas blew through the city, making it perhaps only 10 degrees. It was raining, too. I thought people came to Miami at that time of the year to relax on the beach. Maybe they did, but they would have needed an umbrella. Such a low temperature on this leg of the journey boded ill. It had been cool in the Andes but I'd ridden a bicycle to keep warm. Now I had only a tent and a sleeping bag. I tried not to think about what lay in wait further north.

The road leading away from the airport also grabbed my attention; there was no sidewalk. More concerning, the boulevard was overgrown with juniper bushes, leaving me to plod along a narrow shoulder on a busy road. Cars sped by and splashed through puddles, soaking me. Horns honked for me to get out of the way. I tried thumbing a ride, but there was nowhere to pull over even if someone did want to give me a lift. I had romanticized the idea of hitchhiking across the States as my travels in South America drew to a close. Now, putting foot to pavement, my blueprints for getting home blew absurdly in the breeze.

Worse, other than heading north, I didn't know where I was going. Itching to bolt after clearing immigration, I did not stop at the airport

3

info centre to ask for directions. The faster I was out of sight, the better; I didn't want to give the entry-stamp people time to change their minds. I hoped to find a map at a convenience store. Maybe I would luck into a ride without having to tough it out on the freeway. I had walked two miles with these thoughts still making their rounds when a State Trooper pulled over to check me out, lights flashing. I got a familiar sick feeling and put down my bike bags slowly, just as the cops were getting out of their car.

Gone daddy gone, the love is gone away. – VIOLENT FEMMES

Hitchhiking had come about by misadventure, not as part of the original idea. I'd envisioned a much longer bike ride: through South America and all the way back to Canada. A two-year stint as a bike courier in Vancouver triggered the scheme. Ripping down city streets and weaving through traffic spurred me into shape. The job, with its constant thrust into streams of moving vehicles, also evolved into a reliable source of adrenaline rushes. I worked alongside some zany riders – dozens of kindred cycling souls who constituted what some of us thought of as a subculture. Rebellious political and environmental ideologies were rife – get out of your car, planet killer! There was verve for fashion: Goths, grunge-rockers and a neo-hippie clown who affixed rubber genitalia to his bike all skidded across the asphalt. After-work gatherings at downtown watering holes were the places to get drunk and talk shop. Most of us had never had a better time making a living.

The drawback was the crashes. Stitches and bloody knees came up every few weeks. I even lost a front wheel once, smashing my face open and incurring a major concussion. But the fire to ride still blazed and I ignored the injuries. That changed after a year, as the whole gig slid into punch clock boredom: Being a bike messenger made few mental demands. Such 9-to-5 emptiness launched me into daydreams about South America.

5

As the months stacked up, one courier or another would return from an exotic place like Thailand or India. Listening to them tell of their travels over a pint moved me to vibrant rumination. Packaged tours or smoking a hookah with slumming jet-setters sounded like a welcome break, however bland. For contrast, I began tracking the world's most dangerous places. Some of the hotspots were in Latin America. Having just spent two years sweating myself into condition now propelled me toward countries listing on the brink. Besides, I needed a sharper edge than bike couriering to raise body and soul to a higher level.

Recklessness wasn't my only motivator. Politics played a role. The arms race in the 1980s scared the hell out of me along with the rest of the world, waking me up to a plenitude of other disasters in the bargain. Coups d'etat in Latin America, the Iran-Contra affair and civil war in Lebanon were standard-bearers in a parade of fear and instability. I watched these things from a safe distance without probing deeper. I knew only that fortunate souls in rich countries lounged in coddled safety as wars and famine raped the worst-off sectors. I needed to get to the place where flesh met ruin.

But the strongest pull had to do with my upbringing in suburban Vancouver. Middle class life in the 1970s was soft. My childhood abounded with privileges: swimming lessons; enrolment in a soccer league; summer vacations and an embarrassment of presents under the tree at Christmas. I revelled in all that stuff, but none of it could hide the rot that tore my family apart. I'm not sure if my dad started to drink in earnest when his law practice began to fail or the reverse.

He had always liked booze. I didn't know how much until one Saturday morning during the ride to my soccer game. I played for a team of 10-year-olds called the Red Devils. Other than showing up to games and practices, one further responsibility remained: Each team member was in charge of bringing cut oranges for the rest of the squad to eat at halftime once during the season. I reminded my dad to buy some a week in advance of our turn. The night before the game, he poured a scotch and said he'd pick them up in the morning.

The games were always early, with kick-off usually before nine o'clock. My dad never liked mornings but he always got out of bed to take me. My mom came to most of the games too, dragging my sister along, but for the years I played soccer, ferrying me to and from the field was my dad's biggest contribution to parenting.

That particular morning it was only the two of us. I was shocked that he didn't put on any clothes or comb his hair – he just threw on a housecoat and we roared off in his '63 Buick Riviera. He carried along a thermos, even though he didn't brew any coffee to put in it. We were nearly at the soccer field when I mentioned the oranges again, and my dad swerved into a supermarket parking lot on the next block. He nearly fell through the entranceway and, after blankly perusing the aisles, filled a plastic bag with a dozen oranges. I had to stop him before he made it to the exit.

"Dad, we have to pay for them first."

"Oh, right."

At least he'd remembered to tuck his wallet into his housecoat.

We got back in the car and on the road when another problem arose.

"Uh, dad?"

"Yes?'

"They're supposed to be cut into pieces. We don't have a knife."

"Why didn't you tell me that before?"

"I did. They cut the oranges that way every week. I thought you saw that."

"Well, these will have to do."

At the field, I ran away from my dad's car, hoping one of the other parents would see the oranges and somehow get them sliced. The Red Devils were down a goal at halftime and the coach wanted to know whose turn it was to bring the fruit. I told him it was mine and looked for my dad. He was drinking from his thermos, apparently having forgotten about our trip to the grocery store. Cringing with dread, I called for him.

7

"Dad!"

"DAD!"

His booming voice echoed across the field.

"YES?"

"We need the oranges!"

He lurched across the soccer pitch with the bag of uncut fruit, housecoat blowing in the breeze. My teammates stared. The coach shot him a perplexed look, and then distracted the players by talking strategy. My dad clumsily handed me the bag and offered some encouragement.

"You're only down a goal. Five bucks for the guy who ties it and 10 for the guy who scores the winner."

"Thanks," said the coach, "I'll take it from here."

As my dad headed back to the sidelines, one of our midfielders began to complain.

"Hey! These oranges aren't cut."

The left-winger bellyached, as well.

"Yeah, how come you didn't cut 'em? We can't eat 'em like this. I want an orange slice!"

I was peeling by hand as fast as I could, but the skins were too tough. The referee whistled in the second half.

Our opponents blew two more quick goals past us before we got one. With 15 minutes left in the game, they popped in another, making it four to one. My dad tried to rally the team, starting with special abuse for me.

"Get your head out of your ass and your mind out of neutral! We need three goals!"

I ran down the field, humiliated. Why was he yelling at me anyway? I played defence and had never scored a goal in my life. He bellowed some more.

"At halftime it was five for the tying goal and ten for the winner! Now it's 10 bucks for each goal until we tie it and 20 for the winner! C'mon Red Devils!"

I threw a sideways glance to the scene off the field during a stoppage in play. Some embarrassed parents chuckled at my dad. Most gave him a wide berth. A few gawked in disbelief.

When the final whistle blew, the score hadn't changed and I retreated wordlessly to the Buick. From that day on, I feared what my dad would do on the sidelines. Sometimes he was quiet. Usually he delivered a mortifying harangue. Not long afterward, my dad unravelled completely. He would walk around the house in my mom's underwear. I also saw him in her mini-skirt. By then, my dad was drinking constantly: rye, scotch, vodka and beer. His secretary worriedly phoned my mom to say he'd been drinking himself unconscious at the office. My mom said he was losing business and we were going broke. He started locking himself in our laundry room for days at a stretch, not coming out even to eat. On the rare occasions my dad emerged to defend a client in court, I'd go through the room and find his hidden bottles.

Soon enough, my dad drank his way out of the family and into oblivion. But he still cast a menacing shadow from his rented basement suite two blocks away. Once the divorce proceedings got going, he would drive through the subdivision in a drunken fog, scaring the neighbourhood kids. He also broke into our house at night. Twice, I watched him skulking outside in his housecoat, his hair in its familiar shaggy, upturned mess. I never saw him enter, but my dad must have jimmied a door; my mom had changed all the locks after he moved out. I could hear him downstairs most nights, but tried to blow it off as imagination. I wondered if my mom and sister did the same.

One night my mom pulled down the blankets on her bed to find shards of broken glass. She held off calling the police, hoping my dad's malevolent nuttiness would end there. She also wanted some normalcy in the household, despite the intimidation. My mom was moving on. She began to see a man she had met at work. The guy had an uproarious sense of humour and my sister took to him right away. He cracked jokes and treated us to movies, but I was sullen and never comfortable with him.

9

All the while, my dad continued to oppose the divorce, getting furiously drunk and blaming my mom for everything. He had been slightly acquainted with her new boyfriend before the two were romantically involved, and now added him to his shitlist. One Saturday night during his wanderings in our house he kicked down my mom's bedroom door, ranting.

"Move out of the way you fucking bitch! I'll smash you and that kinky-headed fuck into a bloody coma!"

Listening in fear and praying he would go away, I took some solace that my sister was sleeping over at a friend's place that night. But it became too dangerous for any of us to stay at the house, even after my grandpa fitted the doors with steel bars. My dad had a sawed-off shotgun. When my aunt and uncle went to tell him that his mother-in-law had died, they found him drunk, with two rifles laid on his bed. He explained to them that he kept another rifle in the trunk of his car and was planning to kill my mom.

The three of us left town after that, but the bad times had exacted an immense toll. My sister fought hard and rode out the storm in our new location, but I had too many character shortcomings to bear up. My dad's horrifying and total collapse filled me with immense rage and shame. By the time I turned 14, I had escaped into an umbra of pot and booze. The next year I disappeared into an alternate realm of psychedelics.

Ten years of fights, drunk tanks and confused romantic entanglements followed, edging me toward the nadir of self-destruction. Even so, I faked a measure of stability. I finished high school, got a job and, once I hit legal age, kept out of trouble with the cops. But by twenty-five the drunken pointlessness of my life had become a thoroughgoing embarrassment. I had made things more palatable by spending most of my time downtown, where the distractions were plentiful. Still, I knew nothing worth knowing. That is unless you count a vague awareness that I'd contributed to the privation of people in poorer countries by taking up more than my share. I wanted redemption. I also had to know if I could overcome the soft toxicity of my early years – or at least find a less predictable road to death's door.

Who can tell what waits beyond this road? I'm a drifter, a lonesome drifter. – JOHNNY CASH

Still fighting to leave the worst years behind, I bought an airplane ticket to Mexico, carting along my bike, tools and panniers. The panniers made it through two jungle excursions while my bike did not. That day in Florida, I gripped the familiar acrylic straps that bound them shut as the cops drew closer.

"Let's see some ID."

One of them took my passport and padded back to the car. I stood ten feet from the other patrolman. Neither of us had anything to say. The first cop returned five minutes later.

"Where are you going?"

"Vancouver."

"Where?"

"Vancouver. It's in Canada."

"What're you doing on the highway?"

"I'm hitchhiking."

"That's illegal in Florida."

"The immigration people didn't have a problem with it."

"That's because they deal with immigration. I deal with people once they get on the highway."

I could tell the cop was angling for an out. He had just checked my passport, which hadn't generated any red flags. My immigration stamp was fresh and I wasn't offering up any lip. He had better things to do. Still, he needed a plausible alternate plan from me. I made one up for him.

"Where is the bus depot?" I asked.

"It's in town. If you walk up to that intersection and keep right you'll get to where you need to be."

I thanked him and watched the cruiser roll away. With the money I had, I couldn't afford a bus ride to Alabama, let alone make it home. Walking ahead, I considered the hold-up worthwhile. I now had some valuable experience in dealing with American cops.

A convenience store appeared across the byway after another mile. I did some arithmetic before selecting a road map from the display counter, having no idea how long my 75 bucks would have to last. Two weeks sounded like a good guess. The booklet, food and a drink set me back ten dollars, leaving me just under five a day for a 14-day trip home. I set my purchases on top of the garbage can outside the store and tore the plastic wrapping from a steaming hot burrito. The map showed the shortest way north was along Interstate 95, hugging the East Coast of the state.

I ought to have guessed the highway would be easier to locate on the map than on the ground. Almost no one I asked for directions could speak English; I had forgotten that Miami has a large Cuban population. Despite just having returned to North America from a largely Spanish-speaking continent, I'd made little headway with the language beyond "Where is the bathroom?" and "Where can I buy beer?" Linguistic nuances such as "Where is I-95?" were beyond my grasp. Later, I encountered a man with a Caribbean accent who told me to make a series of lefts and rights until I arrived at Okeechobee Road (he hung onto the 'o's in the word: "You be lookin' for Ooohhkeechooohhbee Rooooad, mon"). From there the highway would be easy to find.

My luck improved when two guys in a van saw me on the road and stopped. They were a couple of jovial Cubans with a cooler of beer in the back of their TV repair vehicle. One of them passed me a bottle of Corona and asked me where I was going. Both men laughed when I told them I was heading to Canada. Didn't I know it was cold up there? They were intrigued, and asked me how I came to be on Okeechobee Road. Part way through an explanation, the driver pulled over to let me out. They had to turn off, toward a residential area to fix a TV. The ride had lasted 15 minutes. I downed my beer, and they wished me well as I hopped out of the van, bolstered by the brew.

The road led to an onramp, funnelling cars onto the highway. The thoroughfare was a depressing sight. I stared in hopeless wonder at eight lanes of speeding traffic, and thought back to some of the sleepy highways in British Columbia where trying to get a ride wasn't so daunting. From a hitchhiker's point of view, Interstate 95 was a disaster. The shoulder was a thin strip of gravel that permitted negligible walking space. There was nowhere to pull over, and a deluge of cars and trucks whizzed within five feet of me.

An hour of thumbing time remained before sundown, and I stood rooted to a spot where an adventurous motorist might stand a chance of pulling over. But drivers hurtled along the highway, disregarding me as though I were one of the crushed bugs on their windshields. I'd never felt so insignificant. Thoughts of a long trip home crossed my mind as I walked off the Interstate minutes before dark. I'd had enough for one day. Besides, I needed to find a place to hole up for the night.

I'd stayed in some grimy hotels in South America. For two or three dollars, you could find a basic room with a shared toilet – generally pictures of squalor with undrinkable water. All the countries I visited were home to cockroaches the size of a package of cigarettes. At night you could hear them scuttling across the floor. By three in the morning, you had to flick on the light to sweep eight or ten roaches out of the bed. Rustic sleeping arrangements were nothing new, but all I-95 had to offer was a slim boulevard with minimal bush cover to conceal myself from passing Highway Patrol officers. I selected a spot between two trees that someone else had used before. An empty tin of beans sat next to a dead fire pit, and a faint smell of urine emanated from somewhere close. I hoped this wasn't the regular haunt of a local tramp.

I pitched my tent with a grumble. I was cold and hungry. I tried to get some sleep but stones and broken glass on the mud beneath the tent jabbed at me most of the night. Just as distracting was Interstate 95 itself; the thoroughfare was an unceasing convoy of eighteen-wheelers. The trucks plied the roadway in both directions at all hours and I woke up whenever one passed in the lanes closest to me. The sound of acceleration pumped out of the mufflers at ear splitting levels, and the smell of diesel exhaust was all encompassing.

Early the next morning, I prepared to get rolling. Basic grooming proved no easy task, as the space between the bushes offered limited privacy; I was even able to make out faces in passing cars. Supplies were low. I had purchased a tube of toothpaste a month before in Ecuador and still had a squeeze or two left, but there was no soap or deodorant. All my clothes were dirty. It had been days since I'd washed my hair, and a week's worth of beard sprouted on my face. I hoped to flag a ride before anyone got too close a peek at me. None of the drivers cruising past seemed to notice the strange figure moving about on the boulevard. That was good; I didn't want to attract attention until I found a spot with lots of room for somebody to pull over.

A short walk led me to an auspicious-looking shoulder. I stood there, mulling over the two techniques normally used when thumbing a ride: walking and waiting. Hitchhikers walk for all sorts of reasons. For example, on sunny days it's enjoyable to set a pace beside the highway, and on cold days a walk can shake off the chill. But the most important thing is to get moving. The key premise of most walkers is

16

that, even if nobody stops to pick them up, they'll make it under their own steam. That design typically fizzles into bankruptcy when there's a whole continent to cover.

The other problem with walking is that it can put the hitchhiker out of position. The walker continually needs to turn to face vehicles and extend a thumb. This is a pain in the ass. It's also easy to miss rides that way. In the long run, the motion of spinning around and trying to focus on oncoming drivers produces a blurry nausea. I once even twirled right into a highway sign in front of a carload of giggling young women who then declined to pick me up. That performance taught me the importance of eye contact. It allows the driver to size up the hitchhiker from 100 feet away, and many have told me they stopped because I looked them in the eye. Walkers who trudge ahead with their thumbs out and their backs to traffic drastically lower their chances of getting a lift.

Long distance hitchers who patiently wait assume a ride is coming. If the hitchhiker finds a wide shoulder beside the road, it is a good idea to wait there; so much the better if there is an onramp where cars are not yet up to highway speed. Either way, a car will stop eventually; it may just take all night to get there. Waiting can be boring, but it is almost impossible to avoid some tedium while hitchhiking. I subscribe to the waiting theory: Staying in one spot ensures you'll never be caught out of place.

So I waited that clear and cold January morning, still only 20 miles outside of Miami. As it turned out, I didn't need to exercise much patience before an ancient Valiant stopped. The thing was in rough shape. Rust covered the exterior – not a scrap of the original paint job remained. Shredded upholstery was the only vestige of a former backseat, and frayed threads hung on to chunks of seat stuffing up front. The engine sputtered and a section of rope almost held the driver-side door in place.

The lone driver was about my age, very thin and spoke no English. He introduced himself as Pedro. Employing my feeble Spanish, I dis-

covered he had come from Cuba six months before and that he was
driving to Northern Florida to see his uncle. He said I could ride with
him that far – though it was improbable the Valiant would actually
get there. Still, this was a major stroke of luck: One lift might get
me almost clear of the state – maybe I'd overestimated the length of
the journey home. I stretched out, peacefully meditating on the long
cruise ahead.

The interior of Pedro's vehicle wallowed in three feet of sundry
crap. The top layer was all fast food bags and candy bar wrappers. I
couldn't tell what the lower levels were, but it didn't matter – I could
put up with slovenly habits for a lift to Northern Florida. Pedro's personal grooming contrasted with the condition of his car. His button-
down shirt was nearly threadbare, but pressed and clean, tucked into
a crisp pair of trousers and belted. He had also recently scrubbed up,
washed his hair and cut it conservatively short.

Pedro stopped at a gas station and pulled out two crumpled one-
dollar bills. He wanted me to run in and grab some sodas for the
trip. Not having had breakfast, I nearly drooled at the prospect of
sugar and caffeine. We chugged Pepsi, sounding like idiots, trying to
make sense of what the other was saying. He presented as easy-going,
and just glad to be in the country. I gathered Pedro had immigration
problems when he kept repeating a sentence that ended in "USA."
Recollections of the bare government rooms and uniformed drones
at the airport turned my stomach. Pedro definitely had my sympathy
if he needed to deal with any US officials.

The decrepitude of Pedro's car added to the charm of the ride.
What were the chances I'd have found myself cruising up I-95 in a rat-
tletrap that would have probably looked more at home in downtown
Havana? Slim, I thought. But the brakes were slammed on those giddy musings when the old car cast up a sucker punch of a secret. The
lock on the Valiant's glove box popped open and a picture fell out, a
shot of a boy about eight years old, clothed only in a pink G-string.
The youngster was unconscious, with a lolling tongue and splayed

limbs; it looked like he had been drugged. I gaped at the photograph. When Pedro saw what had dropped, he grabbed at the picture, fumbling three attempts to snag it.

He turned it over and held it. Neither of us spoke, sweat beginning to form on Pedro's brow. I felt sick. Pedro drove five more tense minutes before pulling over. He mumbled something in Spanish and pointed to the door. It was obvious to both of us the time had come for me to get out. I grabbed my stuff and obliged. The Valiant coughed, jerked back onto the highway and headed north. I thought fleetingly of letting the law in on Pedro's picture, but tossed the idea. I didn't relish the notion of having to explain my mode of travel to any more cops – a topic sure to come up for discussion. Nor did I think anyone in law enforcement would seriously consider a tip from a guy in my position. I moved up some distance, and then stood at the side of the road.

A guy in a 5-ton truck stopped before long, heading toward Tampa – a ways off from the route I'd picked, but it was all the same to me. He was going north. First we motored west on Interstate 75 through the Everglades across a corridor called Alligator Alley. The moniker turned out to be a tease; the alligators, if there were any, had hidden themselves among the lilies and grassy expanses. Airboats with huge propellers dotted the dry docks along the circuit. The boats sat in parking lots, looking like rows of oversized house fans in a hardware store.

The driver didn't say what he was hauling and I didn't care to ask. He wore a new Tampa Bay Devil Rays cap, so it was no surprise that he wound the conversation around to baseball. A franchise had been awarded to the city a year before, though the Devil Rays weren't slated to throw their first pitch for two more seasons. The driver loved to talk about it. He lived in a Tampa suburb and planned to go to a bunch of games, "even if the team had more niggers on it than white boys."

I recoiled.

"Just about all the crimes in Tampa are done by niggers. Damned if we need 'em on our baseball team."

I had heard the word "nigger" uttered enough times, but it always came as a shock. My Canadian naïveté had given me the impression that casual use of the slur had become outmoded after the 1960s Civil Rights era. Hadn't enough changed so that no one except rappers and the few remaining Klan members used that ugly relic of a word anymore? We were going all the way to Tampa. I squirmed, not knowing whether it was smarter to keep going or to ditch the ride. I tried to tune the guy out, staring at the highway. There were armadillos sleeping on the side of the road, bunches of them curled into rounds.

Ignoring the trucker wasn't working. My mind raced. I could have called the cops earlier when I found out about Pedro and his kiddie porn jalopy, but I had decided against that. I could still have redemption of a sort; now was the time to say something. Rationalization set in: It was high risk for minimal chance of payoff. I might have to wait overnight for another ride if he kicked me out, and I doubted the driver would change his views if I opened my mouth. Maybe he would listen, but I didn't have the stomach for it. Hungry and starting to crave liquor, I thought of my pathetic cash supply. I would struggle not to fork over a few bucks for a six-pack that night. I needed to keep moving.

Later on, we stopped at a store southeast of Tampa. I restrained myself from perusing the beer cooler and bought a coffee and a tin of black-eyed peas instead. My heart nearly stopped as I approached the till. The truck driver had a case of beer tucked under his arm. Cold Miller. I could nearly taste it. I burned my throat guzzling the coffee too fast in a fit of nerves. Back on the road, the trucker said he knew of a ravine that hosted bush parties and dirt bike races; it would be a good place to set up my tent.

Empty beer cans and condom wrappers littered the site. Plastic motor oil bottles and pizza boxes filled old fire pits, but the ravine was deserted. I pitched the tent, counting on the trucker cracking open the beer. Luck prevailed – his wife didn't like him drinking at home so we sucked back most of the dozen in an hour-and-a-half. The brew soothed my scalded throat and eased my nerves. This was the life, I thought, slurping my fifth beer. Yessir – drinking with a redneck in a Florida backwater wasn't without its merits. Even so, I couldn't blot out anger for the way he talked about black people. I choked back disgust with myself for not speaking out and returned to drowning in beer. The truck driver ruined my liquid escape when he took the last two bottles of Miller and stuffed them under the front seat of the five-ton. I wanted one more. He said goodbye and drove off with the beer.

The sky darkened ahead of a rainstorm moving up from the south. I pulled out my Swiss Army knife to open the can of black-eyed peas. Amused at seeing the legendary Southern staple for the first time, I set down to supper. The peas were okay, but I couldn't understand why they were so popular. Maybe they were better cooked. I sat, chewing, knowing I had become a ride-whore.

A slight hangover and the pouring rain threw me off-kilter in the morning. The two-mile walk to the freeway exit soaked me to the skin. It was still early but the low sky was black as night. It rained so hard the drops felt like a rubber mallet hitting my head. The rain fell continuously for the four hours I spent waiting for a car to stop. When a ride finally materialized, it turned out to be a short one. The man who picked me up was well-dressed and in his late 40s. His car was new and clean inside. He said little, but clearly felt sorry for me. I reeked of stale beer, and was so wet that I must have left a water stain on his seat.

I fought depression as the man dropped me off half an hour after picking me up. My fingers were prunes and everything in my bags was drenched. The longer the day wore on, the louder the traffic sounded, and the more the constant hissing of tires got on my nerves. On two occasions, nasty bastards swerved into puddles close to where I stood, spraying rooster-tails of bilge water on me. I-75 splashed like a writhing snake with no beginning or end. Three hours passed before my next ride.

There is no more relieving sight to a cold, exhausted hitchhiker than brake lights. Seeing a car slow down and pull over can raise sagging spirits in a hurry. The beaming taillights on the late-model Grand Am had just that effect, as I watched it stop. I nearly cried at the prospect of getting out of the rain, not daring even to hope for a long ride or a warm-hearted driver. Part of the excitement of hitching is the complete mystery of who's inside the vehicle. On that day, I wished I knew more before jumping in and closing the door.

The interior of the car was spotless – so was the dude behind the wheel, unnervingly so. He wore a brand-new house painter's smock; it was white and unzipped, exposing the label of a designer shirt. Good-looking and about thirty-five with a chiselled jaw, his haircut must have run 200 dollars at an upscale Miami hair salon. The presentation was wrong, but we were moving before I could rethink this deal. More off-putting was the twitch. The muscles in his neck pulsated and clenched. They ticked when I thanked him and again when I introduced myself after an awkward silence. Whenever I spoke, his neck contorted. Following another long pause, I managed to wring out his destination: A town called Hilliard in Northeast Florida. He was planning to "visit someone" there.

He'd pencilled the town on a road map, and would drive north past about 70 exits before cutting east. Glad at the prospect of staying out of the downpour, I tried to initiate conversation, probing for details. But my efforts irritated the driver, and he answered tersely, eyes wide to the road. His mouth screwed into a grotesque purse and he twitched spasmodically. Only the whizzing sound of rubber on wet asphalt met my other questions; we had embarked on a communications blackout.

Searching for any useful information, I noticed that the car smelled like it had just rolled off an assembly line. That, combined with the driver's glittering haircut and weird overclothes, somehow gave me the impression he was trying to outrace the past. I guessed he wouldn't talk because he had deleted any sense of his own history. He definitely struggled with the present. I don't know if it was the heater in the car or worry that my amateur head shrinking was on the money, but I started to sweat.

He began to speed. Then he weaved in and out of traffic 30 miles an hour too fast. Through the windshield, headlights and taillights blended into a watery glow underneath the pelting rain. I held on, agonizing, before he eased back to the speed limit. Seizing a moment of apparent safety, I asked him what he was planning to do once he had made his connection in Hilliard. Immediately, his neck spasms returned. He said nothing. Instead, he slowed right down and pulled over on a gravel shoulder. My rough count of exits we'd passed put the number at around 15 – far short of the 70 he had spoken of clearing. I asked him what we were doing there.

"I'm just going to get something out of the trunk."

"Uh, like what?"

"Something to help me find my way north."

"Your map looks like it'll do the trick."

His eyes narrowed and his throat squirmed like a serpent.

"I need to get something else!"

I grabbed my soaking panniers, jumped out of the car and told him I'd walk. Eyes bulging, veins standing out at his temples, he screamed,

"Get your ass back here, you hitchhiking fuck! I'll take you where you want to go – come back here, you piece of shit!"

Already speed-walking away from the car, I made sure to carry my panniers with their glow-in-the-dark tape facing oncoming traffic. More than anything, I wanted other drivers to see me. I covered 100 feet and turned. His trunk was open, one hand resting on top of it, the other part way inside. I could make out nothing of the contents. His twisted grimace radiated insanity, white smock now spattered with rain. Our gaze remained in stalemate for a long minute.

Then he slammed the trunk shut, jumped in his car and squealed his tires back down the highway.

Wet and shivering in the dark, I said a grateful prayer that my jugular hadn't been slashed. Rain pattered my tent as I lay inside, next to a set of train tracks.

Happiness is a warm gun. – BEATLES

The heat in Latin America made sleeping in the tent nearly impossible, but packing it along saved money for a short time because I usually had to set up outside of town. That kept me away from bars, as well as the temptation of an easy night in a hotel. I grew to tolerate the portable sweat lodge, as it also served as a garage for my bicycle. I would stretch it over the bike and peg it into the dirt. The contrivance protected my ride from thieves, but it took up half the floor space, forcing me to sleep looped up like a question mark.

There were other sources of insomnia. Most of the countries I travelled in did not use daylight savings time; full darkness arrived at seven o'clock. Poring over books by flashlight burned out too many batteries, and the material I had went largely unread. I'd swat mosquitoes and stare at the sky for hours unless it rained. During nights spent on the Mexican shoreline, I could see electrical storms flaring who knows how many hundreds of miles across the ocean. It made for a brilliant show, one so distant that I heard no thunder.

The police also helped keep things lively after sundown. 'Security checks' were commonplace, as were general searches. Three cops shook me from sleep late one night on the beach north of Acapulco. They grabbed my panniers from the tent and dumped everything onto the sand. Two of them sifted through my stuff while the third demanded to see my passport. They found nothing interesting and shouted at me to get going at first light.

The allure of the tent, with its odd shape and teal-green colouring, was another snag. I'd have it pitched at the roadside no more than ten minutes before a farmer or someone from town stopped to nose around. The questions never changed: Where was I from? What was I doing in El Tuito? I'd shoo them away because I couldn't speak Spanish and communicating by pantomime stressed me out. Residents shook their heads incredulously and warned me about the dangers of the highway.

"¡Señor, la carretera es muy peligrosa!"

I smirked when people told me to watch out for banditos. The local thugs didn't worry me at all. Flush with testosterone, I had come this far south to stare down the basest human malignancies. Bring it, mutherfuckers. Obstructing my zeal was an intestinal disorder that I had picked up in Acapulco. It caused incendiary diarrhea, busting headaches and persistent light-headedness, like when you get up from a chair too fast.

The sickness wore me down on the scorching Mexican coast. Riding became unworkable and I took a bus from Puerto Escondido to Tapachula, at the Guatemalan border. A compassionate Dutch kid named Michael kept an eye on me. Often too dizzy to stand up by myself, he helped me get around. Michael oozed with the innocence of sheltered European youth, and he was excited about heading into the Guatemalan highlands to hang out with the Mayan Indians. I had no plans to go that way but, in his perky turn of phrase, he insisted I come.

"Let's go see Quetzaltenango and Lake Atitlán! The mountain air will be a help to you."

Too queasy to protest, I went along, but switched modes of transport with difficulty. The Mexican buses were roomy enough to slide my bike into lower baggage compartments; in Guatemala, only undersized school buses plied the treacherous mountain roads. A ticket

26

secured an impossibly cramped place on a bench seat shared with two other adults. I was the largest person on all such bus rides and wound up cramming myself into the seat with my knees pushed up to my chin. My bike and bags sat tied to the roof, exposed to the heavy rains that came daily.

One exceptionally wet afternoon, the driver charged me full fare to stand in the stairwell of a bus jammed with cages of chickens, tethered goats and farm supplies. The door wouldn't shut because the steps overflowed with people. With only a pole to hang on to, I leaned most of the way out of the bus. Weak and soaked, I could have touched the crumbling highway with my foot if I'd dangled it over the side.

Close brushes with opposing traffic on the straightaway demonstrated there was just enough room to pass. But we had to twist around blind corners on the way to highland towns, and the turns were always cause for panic. The driver would swing the bus into the other lane to hook around, unable to see what was ahead. Oncoming vehicles honked when finessing blind curves. Our guy never returned the favour. Watching as we approached a particular bend, I tightened my grip on the pole. The driver remained cool as the turn drew nearer. Nervous sweat mingled with drenching rainwater as I thought of all the times I'd read headlines like, "Bus Accident in Third World Country – 115 Dead."

We straddled both lanes leaning into the turn, when a horn blast came from just ahead. Another bus, still unseen, was rumbling right for us. Our driver tucked the bus close into the mountainside, nearly launching me out the door and into the rock face. The bus in the other lane occupied an even more perilous position: It had the outside track and a straight drop to contend with if it swung too far to its right. Our bus wobbled as the driver strained to keep the road. The lane straightened and the buses drew parallel, bobbing from side-to-side, grazing one another. The driver didn't even turn around to address the commotion of yelling farmers and clucking hens after he'd made the pass. I hadn't noticed before, but he'd folded in the side view mirror. The driver popped it back into its extended position and pushed on ahead.

I spent two weeks in the mountains recovering from the illness I'd contracted in Mexico. For days, I remained confined to a bed. Michael had wanted to take me to a doctor as soon as the bus stopped at Lake Atitlán. I told him I was only a day or so away from regaining my health and dragged myself from place-to-place, travelling with him all the way to Guatemala City. In the capital, an American nurse gave me some medicine that reduced the light-headedness and calmed my stomach. Even so, the cure was not total, and the condition had sapped my strength. Other than memories of cold, grey and wet mountains, my impressions of the highlands remain fuzzy. When the fever broke, Michael badgered me to accompany him to the Mayan pyramids at Tikal. But I wanted to ride my bike again, south to Honduras.

The uphill struggle that had consumed two school bus-bound days took just over an hour to reverse on my bike. The exhilarating race to the flatlands hurtled me through pine forests and filled my lungs with sun-warmed air. Orchids and other bright flowers clustered at the side of the highway as I neared level ground. I hadn't returned to top form but at least I was back where I wanted to be – the tropics. Only a day's ride from the next border crossing, I unravelled my tent and pitched it, lying there without sleeping until sunrise.

The tenting scheme faded as a viable plan on the night that marked a week in Honduras. The evening began the way many others had. I'd finished eating the staple Latin American supper of rice, beans, beef and plantain, and had set up my tent on a small field 30 feet from the highway. It was twilight when I heard some men shouting. They said the highway was not safe, but I could go with them to camp on their farm. The offer came as a welcome change, though I would not yet admit to myself that the highway was beginning to rattle me. Lots of people had guns in Central America, and every second or third night

I heard shots fired in the distance. I wondered how long it would be before somebody with a gun took an interest in my tent.

The two farmers led me to a dirt lot outside a barn, said good night, and left the well-lit compound. I pitched the tent underneath the brightest lamp, and lay with my head poking out. For the first time I could read at night, and I devoured the pages of a very good novel. But the relaxing time wasn't to last. I jolted upright when boots shuffled over gravel. Shifting position, I could see a silhouette 200 feet away. A man was moving through the shadows. He was carrying a machine gun.

Adrenaline zipped like hot quicksilver, clouding my brain. Was he a thief? More importantly, had he spotted me? I watched as he peered into the chicken coop. Maybe he planned to make off with some poultry. Having set down for the night, I had taken off my runners. The only thing I could think to do was to put them back on. I didn't imagine I would outrun bullets, but in my panic I thought the stranger might refrain from shooting a man wearing shoes. He turned toward the tent as I rustled about trying to find my footwear. I froze with one shoe on, untied, failing to find the other one. In the overhead light, I caught glints of the gun's blue steel – an AK-47. The man said nothing until he came within ten paces of my tent.

He greeted me with the Spanish for 'good evening.' I barely stammered a "buenas noches" in return. The man casually slung the gun over his shoulder and kept talking. I understood about every twentieth word. Shifting the weapon back to his hands, he motioned around the farm with the gun and spoke some more. The terror dissipated as his cadence drifted into a diatribe on some pet theme; the subject matter was a mystery but a man getting on a hobbyhorse is universally recognizable. My eyes glazed as he went on for 15 minutes. He finally stopped talking and walked off. I gathered he was a security guard. Still, I thought, if the security guards down here need machine guns, what must the thieves be using? I shuddered. Bring it, mutherfuckers, indeed.

Crossing paths with Machine Gun Manuel, as I came to think of him, scared me away from sleeping by the roadside in Latin America. I sprang for a hotel most other nights, and the added expense would ultimately force me to shorten my route. But that was okay for the moment: Camping next to the highway wasn't going to work where I was headed.

The name 'El Salvador' still evokes thoughts of the devastating US-backed civil war fought there in the 1980s. Images of death squad massacres, helicopters strafing villages and reports of torture come to mind. In talking to fellow gringos, it became clear that recent history influenced their decision to leave the place off their itinerary. I had marked it as a place of pilgrimage: Crass desire prodded me to rubberneck across El Salvador's wounds. Even so, in my most repressed depths, I hoped that witnessing the country's peacetime regeneration would somehow guide me toward spiritual revival.

I had read of an artist named Fernando Llort who worked in the small border town I approached, called La Palma. Llort's painting technique was famous across El Salvador: brilliant reds, blues and yellows animated simple pastoral and devotional scenes. His brush brightened vignettes of ordinary life in El Salvador, with people often represented as disproportionately larger than their surroundings. Art critics have compared his style to that of Picasso. Riding through La Palma, I saw that a legion of imitators had taken up Llort's method, causing the town to gleam with vividly painted buildings.

The dizzying spin of colours on the shops, houses and murals set against the backdrop of the jungle radiated a lovely, lush energy. On La Palma's main street, the smell of pupusas – fried cheese, onion and meat-filled tortillas – gave my grumbling tummy fits. I stopped my bike and bought eight of them for a quarter apiece. A posse of young Salvadorians eyed me munching the delicious tidbits. One, named Salvatore, asked how far I'd come. His eyes widened; Salvatore had lived ten minutes from my folks' place in suburban Vancouver during the civil war. He said he and his family owed a great debt of gratitude to Canada. Salvatore, his cousin Sandro and the rest of their friends insisted I come along to hang out with them at their uncle's house, where they were staying for the weekend.

The Vancouver connection was astonishing. Even more so was the personage of Salvatore's uncle – Fernando Llort himself. The artist welcomed me with a wide grin and invited me to stay for dinner. At the table, Fernando Llort asked me what I thought of El Salvador and how I liked his art. I had no taste in art but could honestly say I liked the way his work made La Palma a bright place. I also thought it was cool that others had picked up brushes to ape his style, making sure that no flat surface was safe from painters.

After dinner, Fernando Llort poured himself a glass of wine, his fifth or sixth of the night, and asked me to accompany him to his studio. The paunchy and balding greybeard smiled with pride as we descended the stairs to his basement workspace. There sat some finished sketches and paintings, other projects in varying stages of completion. But the thing he most wanted me to see was a photograph of himself next to Pope John Paul II. The pope had stopped in El Salvador years before, during a tour of Latin America. The two men posed for the camera, and now the keepsake, as far as I could tell, was Fernando Llort's most prized possession. I thought I should say something profound about the relationship between art and the Catholic Church, but could think of no comment other than, "Nice picture with the Pope." A deep frown creased Fernando Llort's brow and he briskly guided me out of his studio.

Fernando Llort nevertheless permitted me to pitch my tent on the edge of his property, and I spent the weekend hanging out with Salvatore and his cousins. Salvatore was 17, with a slight build and fond memories of Canada.

"We left El Salvador when the fighting was really bad. Coming to Vancouver was perfect. I never heard any shooting there. And school was great! It only took me six months to learn how to speak English. Everybody there was nice to me. The only thing I didn't like was that you can't get pupusas there and it's hard to find good cheese bread. You can get way better hamburgers in Canada than you can in El Salvador, though."

Salvatore and his mother had gone north in the late 1980s and stayed in Canada for two years. They were sent back home when the war ended, their refugee status revoked. His mom, a sad, soft-spoken woman with bright eyes, still hoped to return but the immigration bureaucrats were stalling on her file.

Sandro and his mother lived with Salvatore and Salvatore's mother in the capital. Humble and reserved, Sandro worked in a bank and spoke little English. He had not accompanied Salvatore to Vancouver. The few things the young man said were about helping his family in a land nearly devoid of opportunity. He delivered his words with intensity and a long stare; I could only guess what it must be like trying to get ahead in a poor country so recently torn apart by war. But he grinned when I brandished a hackey sack, joining his cousins punting it around a circle. Sandro's smile did not go deep, however, and his eyes locked back into far sight after short minutes of play.

Chess was also popular at the La Palma retreat, and a pair of relatives continually hunkered over the board. The rule was that the winner kept playing, taking on challengers. I made the most of my chance, winning until four of the cousins ganged up on me. They strategized together in Spanish, railroading me into checkmate. Not understanding the tongue made me uncomfortable, and I asked for some lessons. Sandro and Salvatore were happy to help out, and I did my best to speak like the Salvadorians as long as I remained at Fernando Llort's place, freeloading for meals. Still, I picked up little Spanish and retained even less of the language.

As the household prepared to head back to San Salvador, Sandro asked me to stay with him for a week. Thrilled at the offer, I stashed my bike in Fernando Llort's truck and hopped in the back seat. The vitality of La Palma, with its artistry in the forests, faded as we drove away from it. The magical aura of the place contrasted with the fact most of El Salvador's wooded areas have been logged. The country's deforestation rate ranks among the world's highest. Sparse stands of mostly oak and pine remain, and the tree deficit erodes the soil.

The grassy hills of the countryside, shorn of all but low bush cover, rolled blandly into the distance. Much bleaker was El Salvador's extreme urban poverty. Dirty, brown San Salvador loomed through the windshield of Fernando's truck. Just like in those 'donate to relieve Third World suffering' TV ads, children rummaged through massive garbage piles on the outskirts of town, a handful of scrawny ragamuffins foraging with heartbreaking determination. On a later excursion through the city core, penniless kids who should have been in school harangued me for the privilege of shining my shoes. One even flung dog poop onto my runner as proof it needed a shine. I slid him a little money and he shot me a broken-toothed smile as he ran toward San Salvador's desolate sector. Long blocks of that city bore as much misery as its poorest citizens. Buildings damaged during the civil war or levelled in the disastrous 1986 earthquake were still in disrepair. Many streets yet retained the spider webs of tremor damage. Worse, everyone breathed the pollution-fouled air. Any more than two hours spent outdoors and you could blacken a clean cloth by wiping it across your forehead.

One night, Sandro drove Salvatore and me to Fernando's house, taking a shortcut through the roughest part of the capital. Sandro warned me not to get out of the car once we hit downtown, where dozens of soldiers, police and plainclothes vigilantes patrolled the streets. Stationed to keep public order, their task was hopeless. Gangsters brawled everywhere. On one corner, a pack of bruisers kicked a man to a pulp, while onlookers sneered at the soldiers. Pimps shouted from cars at the girls working the streets, and every outlaw packed a gun, according to Sandro. The scene rolled past, dream-like, until a beggar screeched an ungodly note, wailing hideously enough to sever body from soul. The cry cut to my marrow, as the streets danced to the weird, ominous glow of people picking their way through garbage fires burning on the sidewalks.

On the margins of the neighbourhood, members of San Salvador's street performing fellowship stood at traffic intersections with mouthfuls of gasoline. One such 'entertainer' nearly set our car ablaze with his fire-breathing routine. The 'Dragon,' as such people were known, lit a match and spit out the gas in hopes of earning a tip. Not knowing of the practice and seeing the flame shoot straight for the car freaked me out. My hosts howled with delight, which did nothing to change my mind that, in San Salvador, I had seen hell on earth.

I stayed two weeks with Sandro and Salvatore. A torrential rain pounded on the day I rode out of the city and water gushed in deep streams down the highway. I pressed on through the storm until I found a cheap place to crash for the night. Hanging soaked clothing from my bicycle, I watched steam rise from my body. The room was no more than a rude cinderblock cubicle in a government park with no shower, and no blankets on the bed. Still, I was back on the road and I never expected anything better than what I had that night. Sandro and Salvatore had warned me to watch myself – that just about everywhere in the country was dangerous. I lay, with a smile, thinking about travel in El Salvador; the place had serious problems to be sure, but it's so small you're never far from where you want to go. It also struck me as ironic that in a country with so much lurking violence, I hadn't crossed paths with any villains – only hospitality.

But the next morning I had nothing to smile about. My front tire had flattened and my clothes were still wet. Once I fixed the tire, stuffed the clothing into the panniers and clipped the bags onto the bike, I could see there was too much weight on the back. The waterlogged gear made it heavier, causing the bike to totter. Such an added load wouldn't have mattered if I'd spent the money on a quality ride – a decent bike can handle that kind of abuse. Second-guessing the decision to economize, I pedalled toward the highway. I had to stop

34

immediately as the case of Montezuma's Revenge or whatever the hell I'd been carrying since Mexico kicked up a serious fuss. Despite feeling terrible, I managed to keep up a reasonably good cheer on that already too hot morning, greeting anyone I saw with as hearty an "¡Hola!" as I could muster.

On a lonely stretch of broken road, two guys walked down the middle of the lane, backs toward me.

"¡Hola!" I shouted.

One of them whirled around. He had a pistol in his hand. The other guy was slower, but pulled a gun out of his waistband before I realized what was happening. I thought for an instant about riding past them, hoping they wouldn't shoot me in the back. But both of them yelled angrily at me in Spanish and I knew it was time to stop. The quick one shouted again and motioned with his gun toward the bushes at the side of the road.

Both men were in their early 20s, and the one giving the orders might have been handsome except for the scabs on his mouth. Our eyes met as I stood astride my bike. The bandito's stance reminded me of an Old West gunfighter: bent at the knees, arms held out from the sides, pistol pointing straight ahead. But the clothing didn't match the posture. Dressed in ripped blue jeans and a long-sleeved shirt with sweat-matted hair, he was probably a farm hand. The highwayman moved as though he hadn't been robbing people for long: He had the gun-pointing thing down but he shook, betraying a sophomoric experience at the trade. Maybe it was his first day on the job. The other guy took up a position next to the road, distancing himself from the main action.

I felt my bowels rumble. My only thought was that I was going to shit myself. Other than the internal movement, I remained stock-still. The ringleader bellowed for me to get into the bushes. I dismounted my ride slowly, hoping somebody would drive past and spook the highwaymen. The scab-mouthed guy grabbed me and stuck the barrel of his gun into my ribs.

He forced me into the bushes, out of sight. The accomplice held his gun to the highway, keeping an eye out for passing cars. There were none. I moved with leaden steps, perspiring and trembling, barely able to control the muscles in my limbs. Incredibly, I thought for the briefest of moments of tackling the robber and grabbing his gun. It might have worked; he was shaking – maybe too scared or inexperienced to fire the pistol. I might catch him off guard. But two guns against none was too great a risk and I chucked the idea. The alpha thug pointed at my panniers. Without hurrying, I began to open one of them. I prayed he'd see a few items he wanted and take off.

The desperado shouted at me to unhook the bags from the bike. I implored in my fledgling Spanish to keep my clothing.

"¡Por favor, señor, mi ropa!"

The gunman fixed my eyes with a cruel stare. He clenched his jaw and bared his teeth, revealing a broken incisor. With an unsteady grip, he shoved the barrel of his pistol into my forehead. I could see the dirt caked underneath the nail of his trigger finger. He pushed the metal hard into the front of my head. Then he lowered his weapon. Up close, I could smell a week's worth of grime on him, and I noticed for the first time that he wore mud-caked rubber boots – almost surely a farmer. In what felt like the frustrating slow motion of a dream, I removed the panniers. Snatching them up, he and his associate sprinted out of the bushes and onto the highway. A car drove up to the roadside. Too stunned to make sense out of what happened next, I watched the two men jump in and split. Had they just carjacked someone, or was the driver in on it? By then the details were irrelevant; I was in a woeful spot.

I picked up my bike from a recess in the shrubs and rolled it to the edge of the highway, standing there like an idiot. At least my bowels had maintained their composure. I was, however, a dude without a plan. There was nothing to do but curse my luck. Later, a metallic groaning sound emerged from the distance. A beat-to-hell pickup truck was heading down the road and I waved at it with madly flapping arms. A farmer sat at the wheel, sporting the sun-drenched complexion of a man in his 50s, calloused hands and a straw hat. He spoke in Spanish and only through gesticulating could I convey what had happened. It was 25 miles to the next town and he kindly let me toss my bike in the back among the sacks of seed and fertilizer.

The gunmen got my clothing, guidebooks, journal and tools. The tent and sleeping bag remained bungee-corded to the rack on my bike, as did the machete I'd bought in Guatemala City. I had purchased the blade for self defense. The irony of the old knife-to-a-gunfight joke sat bitterly with me. Still, the robbery might have been more complete: They could have grabbed my passport. That remained stashed in a money-belt under my shorts, along with 10 dollars' worth of El Salvadoran colones.

I croaked a "gracias" to the pickup truck driver as he dropped me off at the police station in dusty Usulatán. Cinder block offices and jail cells surrounded the cement floor of the open-air courtyard. Locating the chief in a grungy little room, I fumbled through the story. He mobilized a troop of three officers and we sped back to the scene of the robbery in a pickup truck. As the search stretched hopelessly into mid-afternoon, I began to think about the gunmen. Young and poor, they may well have seen some terrible things during the war. Throw in the fact that, while I could afford to travel in the exotic country, they were probably just eking out a living there. Even if they did have jobs on a farm, the work couldn't have paid much. The more I thought about it, the more content I became just being thankful they hadn't shot me. In my mind, I called the exchange even; what choice did I have? A collect call to my sister to cancel my traveller's cheques rounded out the day, and the investigating officers graciously offered me some floor space at the station.

My report had created a short-lived stir at headquarters. But another buzz now made the rounds; that night marked heavyweight boxer Mike Tyson's first fight since his release from prison for a rape conviction. An excited crew of ten police officers pulled up folding metal chairs to watch the bout. One cop, a tattooed, burly guy, would leap out of his chair whenever any of the others walked past the TV screen, pouncing on them and engaging in a mock-boxing match. He even clutched one young officer in a headlock, knocking off his cap. The rest of them sat, laughing, gobbling potato chips and quaffing sodas. I wondered if there was anyone still out on patrol.

Tyson clobbered the overmatched Peter McNeely and the fight ended in the first round. This was a huge disappointment for the police officers and for me; it meant I had to go back to thinking about just what the hell I was going to do. Heading back home so I wouldn't end up dead on the highway was a reasonable option. In preparation for the trip, friends had cautioned against clashing with banditos. Half-drunk and still safe in Vancouver, it was easy to laugh off those sorts of worries. Things were different where the tortilla hit the grill.

But I decided to go on ahead, though I remained in a petrified stupor. My bowel ailment flared in a tectonic way – it had to have been audible from 30 feet. In a sick haze, I inspected my surroundings. The fading afternoon sun revealed two ashen-faced men inside one of the jail cells. I hadn't heard a sound from any of the cages since arriving, and both men remained mute when I unrolled my sleeping bag across from them. I remembered all the times I'd earned a ticket to the drunk tank, pleading my case with the cops as they tossed me behind bars for a night's stay. Never once did I talk my way out of lockup. The forlorn expressions of the men in the cells showed that they had done all the talking that was good for their health. The police usually didn't hesitate to demonstrate that they had heard enough. I didn't even hear the prisoners during the night when I had to get up more than a dozen times, running to the never-cleaned bathroom.

Morning light afforded a better view inside the cell. The two men in shredded clothing were still on their feet, gazing at me in silent despair. There were no cots or benches, and two inches of slime and human waste covered the floor. I didn't know how long they'd been in there or how much longer they would have to stay, let alone why they'd been arrested. But any fool could see that standing up and taking on sleep deprivation was better than lying in that slop. I really felt sorry for those guys.

I set out for Honduras at nine o'clock, with a plan to reach the capital, Tegucigalpa, by sundown. First, there was some business to take care of at the border. The exchange rate for cash at black market frontier posts was marginally better than at the banks. Such transactions were common, but travellers had to make those deals away from prying eyes to prevent government officials from grabbing a cut for themselves. Throngs of calculator-toting cash traders hung out there, shouting after hapless travellers, quoting rates. I'd made these swaps before and now girded myself for another onrush of black marketeers and the packs of beggars that always seemed to follow them. My bus stopped in front of the crumbling depot a few 100 feet from the rushing, muddy Goascorán River. The afternoon sun burned as I rolled my bike toward the rickety wooden bridge that spanned the two countries. An army of moneychangers stood across the bridge. Ten of them ran toward me, yelling,

"¡Señor! I haff best rate!"

"No listening to heem! He hass bad rate. I am giving best cambio!"

"¡No! ¡No! ¡Señor! I guarantee most better than all!"

The men thrust calculators into my face, all showing similar exchanges for American dollars. But with just under 10 bucks worth of El Salvadoran colones to trade, the excitement quickly fell away. As I pocketed a fair deal on Honduran lempiras, the guy I traded with wanted to talk.

"Next time you come back here you making sure you asking for Martin. This iss me. I am needing much more business. I haff many childs and we are poor. You haff some USA dollars to change?"

"No man, sorry. I got robbed near Usulatán. I'm heading to Honduras to get my traveller's cheques replaced."

"You are robbed? This iss big problem in my country. But things are hard here. Many people rob because they too are poor. Iss big problem."

"Yeah, I kinda thought that. Listen man, thanks for the cambio. Better luck with your next customer."

"Yes. Adios, Yankee."

I just waved at Martin without stopping to explain that I was Canadian. Other than Salvatore and his family, most people I spoke with in Central America assumed I came from the States. Some had never even heard of Canada. That boded not so well given all the American military interference in the region. Restaurateurs and shop owners routinely ignored me. A baker even chased me away during my previous stop in Honduras, yelling, "Yankee pig!" As the bus on the Honduran side drove into the mountains, I reflected that, for so many in Central America, the rest of the world consisted of the United States.

The bus wound upward through trash-covered pine forests. Farther into the highlands, the oppressive heat of the lower border area dropped and a refreshing breeze blew through the windows. Late that afternoon, the bus reached Tegucigalpa, just in time to join the fuming rush hour traffic. Divided by the Choluteca River, the capital's economic lines cut along the banks of the waterway. Downtown lay east of the river, with its crowded business district and higher-end hotels. A Dunkin' Donuts caught my eye as we crawled toward a bridge. Crossing over the dirty Choluteca, the bus trundled over potholed streets, bouncing crazily and popping children out of their seats. The stink of sewage hung in the air on the west side of town, but the place also had energy. It jumped with street hawkers, shoe-shine kids and sidewalk booths selling everything from vegetables to crucifixes. At last, the bus pulled into the depot, next to one of the cheapest hotels in town, where I took up residence. A rooster lived in the street below, rousing me early the next morning with a shrill cock-a-doodle-doo.

My folks had bought new gear for me and sent it to Tegucigalpa, which set my mind at ease. But travel costs had reduced my cash supply to a laughable four dollars, now converted to lempiras. By the time

I found the AMEX office on Monday morning, I had only 50 cents. I sincerely hoped no administrative problems would crop up in replacing my cheques. There were a few bad moments when the office doors remained locked until quarter past nine, but when they opened, the man at the counter took care of business. He was a young guy, with a serious disposition. His expression darkened further when I told him what I was doing in Central America.

"We are a very poor country," he said lighting a cigarette. "People are desperate. What you are doing is dangerous. It is only going to get more dangerous the farther south you go."

I had to think about how to respond. I'd been revising my attitude toward the dangers in Central America even before facing those two gunslingers. His warning that things were tougher down the line made me tense up. Even so, I had a genuine smile for him.

"I'll watch myself, man. I figure I can only be so unlucky as to get robbed once on a trip like this."

"Don't be so sure."

Tweeter and the Monkey Man were hard up for cash. They stayed up all night selling cocaine and hash. – TRAVELLING WILBURYS

Too exhausted to think about having ridden with a psychopath earlier in the day, I judged that hitchhiking in Florida was not working out. With nothing dry to change into and my sleeping bag soaked, I spent the night dozing miserably. It rained through the night and I woke up periodically with water dripping on my head. But the skies had cleared up by morning. A cold crispness nipped the air and ice formed on the rainwater puddles. A long hauler's grill sat across the highway and I headed toward it in hopes of getting warm, lured by the smell of breakfast. Crossing the road to investigate, I remained completely oblivious to the fact that the weirdest day of my life had just gotten underway.

Nobody stared at the ragged drifter who slipped past the sign that read, "Please Wait to be Seated." Mercifully ignored, I made for the bathroom and its hot water. Alone in the restroom, I seized the moment to take a 'trucker's shower.' The number of points of personal cleanliness a trucker's shower can improve depends on how much time there is before somebody else walks into the bathroom. I took off my damp and now-reeking shirt to soap down my chest. The sheer pleasure of the hot water splashing my skin loosed a pent-up moan from deep inside.

I grew bolder with the sink as the hot water gushed. Both of my socks were off and I scrubbed my feet in the soapy froth. I was brushing my teeth, wearing only a pair of pants, when the door opened. A truck driver with a long beard and a greasy ball cap stepped into my shower room. I knew that awkward moment was coming. The term 'trucker's shower' is outdated. Lots of truck stops have had full showers for years, and I had my doubts as to whether this particular trucker had ever groomed himself this way. He glared in disgust, but said nothing.

I averted my eyes and kept brushing my teeth, knowing I had to hurry. The trucker's expression hinted that he was mulling over whether to let the manager know what was going on in his bathroom. I grabbed a stall as soon as the trucker finished his business. Keeping an ear cocked for anyone coming through the door, I managed to brush my rat's-nest hair and change into my least-wet clothing before anybody was the wiser.

I decided to skip breakfast at the truck stop and seek cheaper victuals at an adjacent 7-11. Halfway through a stale apple-and-benzoate turnover, I asked the first person I saw if I could catch a ride. The dude said no problem – hop in. This was surprisingly good luck. I even had an opportunity to size the guy up before riding with him. In his late 30s and wearing a cheap-looking bomber jacket, the driver swaggered back to his truck. He wore a pair of knockoff sunglasses and a thick coat of gel in his thinning hair.

He told me he wasn't going far as we cruised up Interstate 75. But he had plenty to yatter on about in the short time I rode in his minipickup, spinning a yarn about having been a Florida Highway Patrol officer a few years before. He and his partner apparently got into a shootout. Under a blaze of bullets, he ran off on his comrade, who then took a slug to the leg.

"I just got scared, man."

I said nothing, having no idea how I'd react in a situation like that. I don't know how the ex-cop took my silence, but he kept talking. He looked edgy. It was as though he'd let a genie out of its bottle and was

44

sweating for a way to get it back in. He rambled into blind alleys and floundered on for 10 minutes before letting another genie out.

He had a side-line on the go. He said he'd been running a drug-trafficking business the whole time he was on the force, having had access to seized contraband. There were rooms holding evidence for cases that dated back years. Nobody would notice if an ounce of cocaine disappeared here, half a pound of pot there. A fellow could make a few thousand a month taking judicious advantage of such outlaw largesse. Fired for running away from the gun battle, he then worked his shady connections into a full-time venture. The trouble was he could no longer pick the low-hanging fruit from the evidence room. He now had to immerse himself in the world of thieves and cutthroats. He knew these people but, as a former cop, he found the trust of the dealers who had the real money slow to come. Result: Three years after his removal from the patrol, he held only the rank of drug mule. But soon – real soon – he was going to make some big deals.

"That, my friend, is absolutely gonna rock! Then these cunts who pick up the dope I drop off can kiss my ass. They'll be working for me. And you know what else? I won't be driving this truck anymore. No way. There's a magazine behind the seat – see if you can reach it – it's got a shot of the '96 Ferrari in the centrefold. Isn't it back there? Damn. Well, I'm sure you know what a Ferrari looks like, but this year's model man – is it something else! The one in the magazine is metallic blue – I've never seen one that colour. I'm getting that model, that colour for sure. You know what that means, right? Pussy! I'm a tit man – and when I get that baby on the road I'll be cruising Miami Beach, picking up babes with fan-tastic tits. Shit yeah!"

The lifestyle of the rich and deluded was only a few moves away. Meantime, he said had to get a load of pot to Dade City. The guy told a tall tale. It wasn't until he instructed me to reach into the console in the back to retrieve a huge bag of weed that I began to see there was more than a bit of substance to his story.

He bragged about how much freight he could get away with smoking before delivering it. I was amazed at the size of the package. There must have been five pounds there. That might not sound like much to someone unfamiliar with the weights and measures of the drug culture. But that cache was probably worth 12,000 dollars. I purposely kept my eyebrows from rising, not wanting to let him know I'd never seen this much pot in one place before. His self-satisfied smirks were beginning to bug me and I knew he was looking for a reaction. The redolence coming from the plastic bags suggested the weed was of an especially high quality. The driver beamed as proudly as any new father. He obviously wanted the stranger in the passenger seat to absorb fully the essence of his illicit ticket to ride.

"Roll us a fattie," he commanded. I was hardly inexperienced in such matters, but wholeheartedly wished he were trucking a load of whisky instead. Nevertheless, I twisted up a joint of considerable girth and passed it to him, thinking about the payload this guy was hauling, and all the cash I'd so recently blown.

I was so heavy man, I lived on the strand. I was so wasted. I was so fucked up." – BLACK FLAG

Money began to vanish as soon as I made the trip from Panama's Atlantic coast to South America. I had sailed on an ocean liner, docking at the old colonial port of Cartagena. Following the gamut of immigration stamps and searches, I biked into the city, invigorated by the salt-tinge of the Caribbean and thrilled to have made landfall on another continent. With the freighters and barges of the waterfront behind me, I wound my way to the banking district to purchase some Colombian pesos. But the banks in Cartagena were closed for the daily 12-to-2 siesta; it was then just after noon. A man standing outside the bank approached me.

"Pesos?"

At first glance, he looked like most of the other moneychangers I'd come across: mid-20s, head on a swivel looking out for police, bouncy stance in case the need to run should arise. Having previously concluded deals of this sort without incident and holding no local currency, I put aside rumours that the Colombian black marketeers were rip-off artists.

I assented with a nod and a "Sí."

Jerking his head, he told me he would "cambio pesos for dollars. Come."

I walked my bike a short distance behind the bank, following the moneychanger. Having just come from Panama with US dollars in my money belt, I planned to trade 30 greenbacks for Colombian cash. The man put the agreed upon sum in my hand when he suddenly appeared startled.

"Policía!" he hissed, glancing toward the corner of the bank before disappearing down the alleyway. I looked around and saw no one. Dismissing him as paranoid, I went to stash the pesos, but instead opened my fist to see that there was only five bucks worth of Colombian cash. Five! Like magic, the bastard had snatched all but one bill out of my hand – impossible! Impotent fury ripped through my belly. The balls it had to have taken to pull off such a sleight astounded me. Boiling with anger and dejection, I rode away with my head down, jaw clenched.

Still livid over my habit of learning things the hard way, I'd regained enough composure to buy more pesos when the banks reopened. That night I tried to put the pilfering behind me as I immersed myself in the splendour of the city's Spanish heritage, drinking wine on the balcony of a restored colonial tavern. Four other travellers joined me at the table, watching the sun sink into the waves. The second bottle of Chilean red wine began to take the sting out of the scam. But I couldn't keep my mouth shut about it. My tablemates laughed.

"But man, everyone knows this place is a rip-off. Why did you go for it?" asked an Englishman.

"I just needed some cash. I'd done it so many times in Central America."

The Scotsman to my left kept saying, "Well, welcome ta Colombia!"

"I won't make that mistake again."

The Scotsman said, "No, but ya shoulda known better. I think we've all heard tha' the thieves in Colombia are like wizards."

I poured myself another glass and looked out at the water. Losing money was easier to take in this beautiful part of the world, enveloped in a wine buzz.

"Yeah," I said, "but I'm enjoying myself now. Look over there."

A young mother and her daughter walked on the opposite side of the street below in white petticoat skirts with red and yellow frills. They had their hair put up in tight buns, noses in the air.

"Oh, that's so cute – they match," said an Englishwoman, reaching for her camera.

The narrow streets of the old city teemed with people. Even over the dinner hour, vendors pitched their cheap jewellery and t-shirts, and neatly groomed children shouted as they kicked a soccer ball. A man pushed a cart, chiming that he had tinto for sale – a strong, sweet shot of coffee. Tourists browsed. A party of well-dressed ladies from town strolled toward our balcony and two men whistled at them from across the street. One of the women turned her head and smiled as she walked on. The sea breeze picked up and curtains billowed from the open windows of powder blue and ochre facades of centuries-old apartment buildings. From our balcony, we had a clear view of the cathedral's spire and the turreted city walls. They dominated the old quarter, embracing the vibrancy of the streets.

The evening ended with half a dozen empty wine bottles on our table. I awoke with a headache, but got up early enough to bolt a breakfast special of pancakes and tinto at a nearby restaurant. The cook was also grilling sale-priced steaks, and I put in an order for one. The meat was cut in a way that I'd never seen before, misshapen and marbled with a network of gristle. Undaunted, I began to devour it; after all, the flapjacks had been tasty.

The steak was tough and not particularly good. Chewing mightily, I pondered what part of the cow this cut would have originated. Knowing nothing about butchery, I couldn't visualize the portion, but thought the animal must have been old and leathery when slaughtered. The more I ate the worse it tasted, and I had to stop halfway.

Queasiness set in as I got up to pay the bill. I asked the cashier what kind of steak I'd just eaten.

"Caballo." Horse. As in, 'I'm so hungry I could eat one.'

49

I stood there stunned, wondering if I should induce vomiting. For three hours the caballo threatened to come back up all by itself. Notwithstanding the zesty union of paddock and kitchen peculiar to the city, Cartagena got dull after a short stay, and I saddled up for a ride to a jungle park farther down the coast. Deep sunburn cooked my back following a shirtless day of cycling. The ill thought-out plan to beat the Caribbean heat failed dismally and layers of skin peeled off. A palm-shaded hammock on a pristine beach was as good a place to recuperate as any, but no more exciting than Cartagena. Idling time was over; the southern highway called.

In two sweltering days, I crossed the coastal plain and approached the mountains. Drinking in the prospect of cooler climes as the Andes rose on the horizon, I foresaw a lengthy ride along the Eastern Cordillera – all the way to Bogotá. The sweat of pressing uphill with loaded saddlebags soon replaced the exertion of biking in the coastal sun. The burden was almost too much at the beginning. Even after shifting to the easiest gear, I strained at the pedals, my legs adapting only halfway through the second day of the climb. By the third day, I became convinced there was no summit to the range.

The lush grasses and palm trees of the plain gave way to jagged rocky outcroppings and cedars as I rode up the switch-backed highway. Deep crevasses gaped at the sides of the road. At the times I stopped for a breather, I would walk to the edge. Usually there was too much cloud obscuring the view to guess how far down the drop went. Once in a while I could see to the bottom a thousand feet away? Two thousand? The longer I rode, the more regularly stretches of flat ground came into view, enabling me to change gears and pedal at a slower pace. On occasion, the clouds would break and stretches of hilly grassland cropped up, clumps of pine and lone oak trees growing on the rises.

Other than the intensely steep grades, the Colombian highway was far superior to anything I'd ridden on in Central America. There were few potholes or major cracks in the pavement, and there were even guardrails at the edges of the precipitous drops. But the best feature was that the road was nearly deserted. For hours at a time, I'd have a misty and cool mountain thoroughfare all to myself. I could hear far in advance when a transport truck approached from either direction, the quiet occasionally pierced by the cackle of unseen birds. The solitude, while it lasted, felt amazing.

I remained contentedly alone with my thoughts and increasingly robust health for long blocks of time; each day on that highway faithfully brought several hours of unadulterated peace. But it also came with its share of headaches. A tire would spring a leak at least once a day. It got so that I could repair a flat in a few minutes, though I always grumbled and cursed under my breath when the latest rupture occurred. My hearing tuned in to more serious bike noises, such as the twang of a stretched brake cable or the ting of a broken gear tooth. When something of that magnitude came up, I swore and then improvised a roadside repair that would buy a fresh stretch of miles.

Just as annoying as the mechanical complications was the consistent attention of the military. The mountain highway hosted a large army presence, presumably to keep the local guerrillas in check. Every day I had to stop at checkpoints manned by heavily armed soldiers; sometimes a transport truck would drive past and pull me over. The stoppages became routine, following a pattern of the highest-ranking guy asking me where I was going, why was I on a bike instead of a bus, and then asking to see my passport.

On Day Six of my journey to Bogotá, the Andes levelled into a major plateau. Through the fog, I could see ranchers' fields scattered along the high flatlands, the odd llama or thin herd grazing. At one juncture where the highway connected to a dirt road leading to a farmhouse, some soldiers were questioning an Indian man. He leaned up against a rough-hewn fence, holding a shovel. The man wore a dark green poncho and woollen pants. He had tied his hair in long, grey plaits. Four soldiers shouted at him as he looked on in silent exasperation.

I craned toward the action, hoping to ride by unnoticed. But a guy sitting in an olive green jeep hollered at me and waved his arms for me to stop. That distracted the other four, who were hassling the rancher. They turned and walked toward me. A man with gold-coloured bars on his epaulettes yelled out an order.

"¡Pasaporte!"

Having been stopped at a checkpoint not an hour before, I handed it over with a glare. The soldier gripped me by the collar and glowered back, then walked over to the others to begin a hushed conference. I made eye contact with the farmer over the shoulders of the huddled military men. He smiled weakly and slipped away, back up the path to his house.

Two guys in uniforms swaggered toward me as the officer who had my passport walked to my bike, now lying at the side of the road. The commander barked again.

"¡Marijuana!" he exclaimed through a bushy black moustache and a gold-toothed grin as he grabbed one of my panniers. But it was weirder than that; he fondled the thing.

Resisting the temptation to roll my eyes and shoot him a disgusted look, I shook my head and said 'no.'

The two junior soldiers stood, smirking, on either side of me as the officer unzipped one of my bags. Then he zipped it back up. He unzipped it again and it looked like he was going to reach inside, but he stopped, flipped my bicycle over so he could reach the other pannier and did his squeezy-feely thing with it.

"¿Marijuana aqui?" he asked.

All of the soldiers laughed. Once again, he undid and redid the zippers and fiddled with the plastic snaps on the bags without looking inside.

"¿No marijuana?"

I shook my head, kept cool and asked for my passport.

The commander snickered and said, "No. Dos horas." I thought he meant I would have to wait two hours to get my ID back. I fumed.

The commander dangled the passport in front of me and then tucked it into his breast pocket, getting more laughs from the troops.

I stood next to my bike for over an hour before the officer gave up the passport, clapping me on the shoulder and uttering a treble-toned laugh. I rode away, but stopped a couple of hours later as dusk approached. The interruption with the soldiers had taken me out of my isolated frame of mind and back into the realm of human contact. I didn't like it. The serene state that came with the exertion of riding alone on the highway was difficult to attain and easy to lose. I grew to love the endorphin-generated sensation that I was strobing with life, and that I was somehow safe.

Such a state was not normal. I attained it every day on that leg of the journey, but only following hours of riding hard along the forested mountain highway. I couldn't get moving fast enough in the mornings, urgently craving respite from panic and depression. That unnamed dread had tormented me for years, though what I suspected were closeted shades of my dad at his drunken worst also allowed me to explain away my own drinking. I had long known I was an alcoholic – a fact I hated to admit to myself let alone anyone else, but denial of the lurking thing that ate away like a parasitic ghost was not working. I didn't drink at all on the ride through the mountains. I joked with myself that that was the problem; despite staying sober, each morning it felt as though I was sick with a punishing hangover.

Riding alone in the Andes, I could keep the pursuing spooks at a distance. At other times, they had needed to be drunk into submission. A week of biking remained before I got to Bogotá, and I looked forward to it. Still, anxiety pressed when I thought of the methods I was sure to use to keep the terror at bay when I got to the city. Despite the grim look ahead, the time that followed was the best of my life; one day I even rode for 100 miles, growing more confident and howling savagely whenever I felt like it. I made brief stops at solitary huts along the highway to buy a cup of mountain-grown coffee, then spending glorious hours on the road without seeing another person.

I became fitter with each passing day. I began to believe I could ride indefinitely – why not just bypass Bogotá? Maybe I could even out-run the phantasms of the past forever.

But as the city lights came into view, I thought about one thing I didn't want to miss: The Platypus hotel. I had heard travellers talking about it as far north as Costa Rica, calling it the coolest hostel in Colombia. The place had a reputation as an oasis for road-weary gringos, sort of a central location in which to recuperate and plan the next move. A Swedish couple I met in Cartagena had stayed there. They told me of friendly travellers, communal dinners and late nights drinking beer. I liked the idea of hanging out in a place with a groovy ambience and talking to people who had been all over South America. I wanted to get a sense of what havoc lay ahead.

Arriving late one afternoon, German, the owner, welcomed me with a cold beer.

"I'm Herman, but it's spelled with a 'G'. It's Colombian. Good to meet you. It looks like you've found a way to see the country up close," he said, glancing at my bike, "make sure not to piss off the army when they stop you, though."

I talked with German for an hour and met a couple of English travellers. But I limited myself to a single beer that night, not wanting to stray from the lofty consciousness that comes only from hammering through the mountains. The exhilaration of that ride stayed with me for a couple of days after arriving at the Platypus. It helped to mitigate the unease of being a stranger. The hostel abounded in cliques, loosely based on national groups. Germans, Israelis, English and a few Canadians gathered at tables in the parlour, chatting in their home language, drinking beer.

I had grown thirsty after the long ride from the coast. Beer at the hotel went for 35 cents a bottle, which was only slightly higher than the prices at some of the shadier local taverns, or so I had heard. Many of the Platypus' guests had recently come out of the southern jungles looking for an econo-bender. By the time my second day in

Bogotá got under way, the excitement of drinking cheap booze and recounting travels after long stretches of solitude on the highway put me into an inebriated mood, too. New faces arrived at the hostel every day and I tried to have a drink with each one.

A cadre of Irish, Danish and Israeli travellers turned out to be my most reliable drinking partners. We discovered a hideout of a bar near one of Bogotá's university campuses. The place was little more than a candle-lit attic, perfect for a night out because the Platypus stopped selling beer at eleven o'clock. Beer prices at the bar dipped below those at the hotel and the rum was cheap, too. We carried on all night and the irresponsibility was as intoxicating as the liquor.

Panic filled the early waking moments of the days that followed. How much money had I spent? Did I wake up the staff again as I stumbled back in at six in the morning? Would German kick me out today? I soon got to drinking as many as 40 beers daily and I shook when I got out of bed. I needed a remedy.

Early one afternoon I opened my eyes, wracked with tremors, when a thick plume of smoke wafted past me. Too sick to drink right away – certain I'd throw up if I had even one beer – I sought out the source of the pot smoke instead. Two men sat with befuddled expression in a room at the far end of the hall. They were part of a crew of seven Israelis who'd just been discharged from the army. I forced a smile: How was a guy supposed to sleep with all this reefer madness going on? One of them snorted and passed me a joint.

It had been months since I had toked. In my teen years, weed had been my daily, hourly companion. I turned my attention to drinking alcohol with a will when I was old enough for the bars, while pot slid to ancillary status. Before departing for South America, I decided to abstain from the stuff for fear of tangling with the law over it. My resolve disappeared that morning and my hand quivered as I brought the joint to my mouth. I inhaled deeply. The taste was bittersweet. Not the best I'd ever smoked, but I was good and stoned when we finished it. I headed to the canteen, feeling better.

The ex-soldiers didn't join me for beer, but I drank with others, talking with people as they walked in and out. By the time I'd had half a dozen, the Israelis came by with another joint. It was a good thing too, as the effects of the first one had worn off and I wasn't sure if I would be able to keep drinking or if I'd get sick.

"Hey there Canada!" said a tall, wiry looking guy. "You look pretty gone. Wanna smoke some more?"

"Yeah, that'd be cool."

"Well come into the courtyard with us – we'll get in shit if we spark it in here."

I followed the troop out of the parlour as one of the men pulled two joints out of a plastic bag that contained perhaps another half an ounce of unrolled pot.

"You'll like this stuff," said a short, pimply ex-soldier. "It's better than what we smoked before."

The Colombian weed worked its curative magic on my rattled nerves. Once again, I felt well.

"Thanks guys – right neighbourly of you."

The Israelis all laughed and headed out the door. They were going to watch a bullfight. I wasn't invited, but tagging along wouldn't have been a problem. I opted for more beer instead.

In the week that followed, I incorporated pot smoking into my boozing regimen. I had never been able to afford to drink this much and my body was rebelling. Pot was the antidote. It kept the shakes to a minimum and allowed me to enter a loquacious circle of potheads. The giddy, ridiculous humour of stoned gringos was just the good time I wanted. Everybody had enough money to keep the party going. Booze flowed freely and nobody cared about anything. The alcoholic nihilism was such that no form of future tense ever entered anyone's speech unless it centred on an approaching need to buy more liquor or weed.

It never occurred to me to investigate the source of the bounteous sacks of pot. It didn't matter. Word was the stuff was cheap and I'd toss in a few bucks if the situation warranted it. There was no need to think any more about it, or so I figured. One morning, during the breakfast six-pack that had become part of my daily wake-up call, a fellow reveller began talking about weed. Apparently nobody had any. That was of little concern to me. My hangover had eased off and I was cruising into a delightful state of drunkenness. But cravings for pot always work their way into your day when you're a regular smoker.

Draining my fourteenth-or-so beer, I felt the insidious desire for dope creep into my lower abdomen. That was where I had usually felt the absence of the anaesthetic as a young burnout. Now the old days were back. My plan was to manage the pangs with more liquor. I was prepared to sit and drink around the clock if necessary. The only trouble was that the cravings intensified with each beer. Good and trashed after putting back perhaps 20 cervezas, I really wanted some pot.

I stammered to some of the drinkers at the table that it would be a good time to score some. They all agreed. It was then I learned the reason for the dry-spell at the hotel: The one guest with a connection was gone. The bastard had checked out without introducing anyone to his dealer. The tone among the boozers had taken on a malevolent edge. A pretty Danish woman swore as she mentioned our former supplier's name. I couldn't remember who he was, which was ironic considering how glaring his absence had become.

The greater irony was that there were eight of us with money to blow on weed – in Colombia's drug hotspot – and no gumption to get any. Everyone at the table knew it was available on the street, but no one had been desperate enough until then to consider making a buy in such a dangerous place. There were thugs everywhere. Without a reliable hook-up, getting ripped off or stabbed was very possible. Even more dangerous were the police. They were notoriously corrupt, and horror stories abounded on the gringo trail of people being caught with drugs and going down for long prison sentences. But our plight was serious – we needed to get high.

All of us had seen the dealers hanging around the grey, rundown buildings a short walk from the hotel. I had passed them many times on my way to the bank or a bar as they stood in doorways. Eyes in that vicinity spotted gringos coming from blocks away. Gloomy, phantom-like types would approach, whisper in Spanish, and fade into alleys, prostitutes gave vacant smiles and roughnecks scowled. We decided who would head down there to pick up a bag of smoke the old-fashioned way: a drawing of straws. Only four of us entered the loser sweepstakes, though the cowardly abstainers would happily smoke the proceeds. It was no surprise to me that I lost the draw.

The rumours of Colombian weed being dirt-cheap checked out; a decent-sized bag went for about 10 bucks. I forced a laugh as all the would-be smokers tossed in 1,500 pesos apiece. The Colombian currency was inflated enough at the time that one American dollar was worth about 1,000 pesos. With all the zeros on the bills, it looked like a serious drug deal was about to go down.

I pushed my chair back from the table with simulated composure, but nearly collapsed on the floor with the first step. I was seriously drunk. The notion of the job at hand churned up an internal chemical reaction, turning my legs to rubber. Combined, the gut-ruining quantities of liquor and massive adrenaline rush made it nearly impossible even to get started. I bashed into the doorframe and staggered into the street.

Pouring rain drenched me before I made it two blocks. I cut a sorry figure approaching Bogotá's skid row, looking down and out even to the street hustlers. Nobody wanted to deal with me – a guy this hammered was a heat score. Dope peddlers skulked away from me as I bumbled in their direction. I knew the longer I spent on the street, the bigger a target I became for muggers and cops. My staggering became even worse and I almost threw up. Oscillating violently, I made it down both sides of the two-block area twice. What remained of my better judgement told me to abort. Still, I entertained the idea of getting stoned, relishing the status as the guy with the skills to bring home the weed. Luck shone a light on me as I tripped into a filthy doorway. A seller was just leaving his apartment.

"Marijuana?" I implored.

He glanced toward the street and replied with a nod. The approaching darkness must have hidden the full glory of my wasted and soaked form. Or maybe the dude didn't care – we were a few steps off the street, and a sale was a sale. I'm sure the hawker dispensed less than a square deal, but the bag looked hefty enough for me to part with the 11,000 pesos I held.

The realization that I was now holding drugs provoked another blast from my adrenal gland. The sickening mix of alcohol and epinephrine whipped my brain into a paroxysm. Six blocks separated the point of purchase from the Platypus' front door – an interminable distance. The pounding rain kicked up vapours from the garbage in the Bogotá slum, stirring them into a horrific stench. My stumbling had not improved any and I was sure I heard footsteps behind me. I dared not look over my shoulder. If it was the cops and they knew I had made a buy, I was screwed. But if they merely suspected it, I stood a chance if I kept moving. My thoughts spun drunkenly out of control; what if the dealer was in league with the cops? I'd heard of that before. The ruse was simple: The dealer sells some dope to a sucker, fingers the mark and the police get an easy takedown. Then they blackmail the gringo's family for as much cash as they can get in exchange for lies about getting off with a light sentence. Meanwhile, the dealer gets his pot back plus a commission. There were whispers of that scam throughout Latin America.

The footsteps grew louder. I wanted to scream but managed to fumble onward. Three blocks now separated me from safety. Hope and piercing terror competed for top spot as I swayed past the greasy chicken-and-fries restaurant our gringo pack frequented. I was close now – the familiar liquor store swam past on the right. The footfalls nearly paralleled my own failing gait. With the hotel in sight, I picked up the tempo, though unable to run. Even if I could have, I would've been easy prey for whoever was bringing up the rear. Half a block now – rain driving as hard as ever.

My hand shook, reaching for the buzzer. I looked behind as I rang. There was no one there.

"Hey! You're back!" declared one of the Bogotá potheads.

"Uh, yeah."

"Did you get some weed?"

I slid through the doorway and collapsed onto a chair, motioning for a beer. Downing half of it at a gulp, I pulled out the bag. Whoops of joy resonated throughout the cantina. It was time to get high. The pot in Colombia was not high-grade by any standard. It could only have been half as strong as the best stuff in Vancouver, but it was so cheap that none of us cared. We rolled corpulent joints, and smoked them while I kept pace with beer. There was talk of heading to the dark little bar with the discount liquor. I don't know whether we made the trip, with the rest of that day now irretrievably lost to alcoholic blackout.

I lost my mind and now my head's a tent and I'm spending time won-dering where it went. – ANGRY SAMOANS

The Florida sun shimmered into the drug mule's truck. A brume of sickly sweet marijuana smoke coiled around the driver's head. He passed the joint. It turned out the ex-cop was moving some serious pot; I was euphoric after four blasts. We had no time for any stoner theorizing, however. The ride ended immediately after we finished smoking. The guy had to turn off the main highway to make his drop in Dade City. He pointed to a truck stop a couple hundred yards away and suggested I ask a long-hauler about catching a ride. I muttered a farewell and ambled toward the restaurant in a pleasurable haze.

A break in traffic opened a path across the highway to the greasy spoon. The place was crammed with truckers, and a fleet of semi-trailers sat parked in the lot. An assortment of company names adorned the transport trucks, though the drivers wore similar uni-forms. All sported jeans that clung tightly to their legs and expanded at the hips, revealing dozens of unlovely ass cracks. A sweat-stained t-shirt (or the occasional long-sleeved effort) caressed their rounded frames beneath nylon workman's vests. Dirty ball-caps, emblazoned with beer slogans or engine parts logos crowned the ensembles that comprised a beautiful American caricature.

Stoned and hungry, I could nearly taste the hamburgers grilling in the kitchen. I couldn't worry about food, though – I had to find a ride. A large sign in the foyer announced "No Hitchhikers Allowed." Undaunted, I lugged my panniers inside. I giggled out loud, concluding that a cardboard cut-out displaying my picture with a red circle and line through it next to the "No Hitchhikers" sign would nicely underscore its intention.

I stood, bemused, for a second too long.

"Table for one, hon?"

The waitress sat me in a booth, placed a menu before me and hustled off to take someone's order. I was going to have to be quick. As she turned her back, I asked the guy at the next table if he was headed north to Interstate 10. He said he was not. I left the panniers at the booth and interrupted 10 more meals with the same question. No, no and no came the replies.

The waitress was moving back toward my table. Our eyes met and her look said that she knew exactly what was up.

"Have you decided?"

"I'll just have some coffee."

"No you won't. You're getting out of here right now."

I grabbed my things and headed for the door without protest. Just then a crazy looking trucker walked in. He was tall and gangly with greasy hair on top of a shrunken head. The tiny noggin overemphasized his pie plate eyes and he kept flicking out his tongue, like a lizard.

"Are you heading west on I-10?"

"No. But if you've got time, I'll get my son to work the C. B. to see if there's anyone going your way. We like to help people get around."

"Hey, that'd be great."

We walked across the parking lot to a semi-trailer cab, and I opened the door just as the driver-side window rolled down. I didn't catch a glimpse of the driver, but grasped that things had taken a turn for the worse as soon as I clambered inside. Floor-to-ceiling, man-on-man pornography plastered the interior. There had to have been

200 dollars' worth of magazines cut up and taped to the walls. My stoned brain tried to assess just how bad this might be as the driver's head still hung out the window, talking to his dad. Then he turned to face me.

I flinched when we made eye contact. My intoxicated bubble burst instantly; he looked just like the inbred banjo player from "Deliverance." The kid in the film never speaks. I wish I could have said the same for the guy in the driver's seat.

"So how old are yuh?" he demanded in a screechy drawl.

"Oh yeah?" he squealed when I told him, "well I bet I been through more shit than you!"

I happily conceded the point.

"I spend my life on the road. So you're trying to get to California?"

Agreeing with him rather than trying to explain fully could only help my cause. He snatched the radio handset out of its cradle and made a pitch:

"I have a 'ham' here. He's trying to get to California. Anyone leaving out of Florida for California?"

He allowed 10 seconds of radio silence before repeating the exact same lines. It was painful to listen to his broken, crackly delivery. But I couldn't complain – he was trying to help and he didn't make a move on me. I sat quietly as he kept on for 25 minutes without eliciting a reply, continually invoking the trucker-speak 'ham' for hitch-hiker, before another trucker told him to get off the air. Just as he was shrugging his shoulders in resignation, his dad jumped in the passenger side, tongue darting madly. I was sandwiched between the two of them. My heart raced as I saw the older man give his son a knowing look.

"No luck with the ride, huh?" the older man asked.

"Uh, no."

"Well, we're goin' to New York. Wanna come with us?"

He broke into a huge grin that threatened to swallow his own meagre head. Distressing thoughts of what might be behind the offer spun through my mind. The fact neither of them made any reference to the copious penis action shots in the cab somehow made the set-up even weirder. I got to thinking it was probably normal for them to pick up hitchhikers with whom to have unspeakable three-ways. I wondered if they had guns or if they would try to overpower me if I refused. I thought of the maniac who dumped me off in the rain the day before. I was petrified. The silence endured for several agonizing heartbeats.

"No."

I crooked my elbow toward the inbred freak, ready to issue a pain-ful shot while staring at the old man. The trucker was crestfallen. I didn't look back to see what the young weirdo was about, but my arm remained cocked. It turned out not to matter. The tension had disap-peared and the standoff fizzled. There was nothing left to do but leave. The older guy swung the door open and stepped down from the rig so I could get out. Nobody said a word as I picked up my things and split.

Still tuned from having smoked with the ex-highway patrolman, I laughed nervously crossing the parking lot; all that panic for nothing. Even so, the scene in the truck had made a demented impression. The idea of a family-oriented, all-guy ménage-à-trois in a moving semi-trailer obliterated any previous notion of sexual boundaries I had imagined – so definitively so that I dared not conjure a vision of it. My thoughts wandered into an even sicker turn: Did father and son simply bone each other on slow nights? Despite morbid curiosity, I feared seeing something I'd regret if I went back to ask.

I found a serviceable hitchhiking spot while considering the truckers' lives of highway driving and buggery. Clouds had moved in and it looked like more rain was on the way. My stomach growled but I didn't feel hungry. In fact, I was energetic. The rush of making it out of that truck unharmed made me ecstatic to be alive. I couldn't recall having felt that way since I was a kid. Or maybe I was just stoned. Doubt worked its way in more deeply with each passing car.

64

Not many passed before a green Chevy Nova rust bucket stopped. My grandfather had owned a similar one and the memory gave me a false sense of comfort. At first glance, the driver looked like a woman but before I got in, I could tell I was about to ride with a transvestite. Under a blonde wig lurked a man in his mid-50s. The dude's impasto makeup failed to smooth a face that resembled a can of smashed assholes. His sweater tightened around two perky, fake boobs. A pair of painted-on pink pants and a lipstick-smeared Kool completed the rig-out.

This didn't surprise me. Drivers in the State of Florida apparently had to demonstrate sufficient insanity, deviance or homicidal tendencies before qualifying to pick up hitchhikers. Running back through the list, I could recall only one or two rides since leaving Miami that hadn't been demonstrably peculiar. I shrugged and hopped inside the old Nova.

I'd known a few crossdressers in Vancouver. They tended to be fun people with their satin dresses, boas and big hair, but this one had critical fashion issues. His ratty canvas purse and makeup held in a plastic Ziploc bag made it clear he couldn't accessorize worth a damn. Worse was the botched attempt to transform his voice into that of a throaty, B-movie femme fatale.

I couldn't help but snicker – loudly.

"What's so funny?" he asked breathily.

"Oh, nothing. I just remembered a good joke I heard this morning."

"Tell it to me."

"No, I think I'll keep it to myself. It's actually pretty filthy."

"I like dirty jokes."

I drew a blank on any punch line that might get me out of that one. At least I stopped laughing.

"Yeah, you really only get it if you're Canadian. It had to do with Quebec Separatists and an ex-Prime Minister. I met a guy from Toronto at the truck stop this morning who told it to me."

"You're Canadian?"

"Yeah."

"You look like a pretty hot guy to have come from such a cold place."

"Right. My grandpa used to have a car just like this one. It ran great."

The driver frowned and asked if I liked his lipstick. I obfuscated again and we drove on for five quiet minutes. Then he wanted to know if I thought a mini-skirt would have been a better choice than the pink pants. I said the pants were just fine, but the hope of avoiding the obvious ended at that moment.

"Well, I'm gay," he said in exasperation.

"Is that so? I wouldn't have guessed. I'm not gay. I hope you're okay with that."

"Most hitchhikers I pick up are turned on by me."

"Oh."

"Yes," he cooed, "they like to touch themselves as I drive. If I like what I see we'll stop and make out. It's wonderful. What are you packing underneath those trousers?"

I wasn't scared but I had to put the kibosh on this.

"Look man, I think maybe you've got the wrong idea. Y'see, I'm just trying to get back to Canada. I'll ride with you as far up the highway as you'll take me, but I'm not going to put out."

He ground his teeth angrily. I almost started laughing again because his expression, through all the pancake makeup, suggested a clown fallen on hard times. Then he laid down the smack.

"Listen, Mr. Freeloader. Maybe you remember those bumper stickers from the '70s? You know, the ones that said, 'gas, grass or ass – nobody rides for free?' Or perhaps you were still in diapers back then. But let me tell you, people knew the rules in those days. You have a choice, Mister: Gimme some or hit the bricks!"

"Like I said, I'm not going to put out."

He jammed on his brakes and we skidded to a halt at the side of the road.

"Get the fuck out," he said with his indignant, caricature starlet's voice.

"Safe travels," I called back, tossing my panniers to the ground.

"Fuck you!" he bellowed before driving off, losing the movie star delivery.

A convenience store lay up ahead, behind some chainlink fencing in a residential area. I walked toward it, purposely not thinking about the day I was having. The store was just a point in the distance; I wasn't going anywhere in particular and I was in no hurry to get there. The sky had darkened and I was not about to try and squeeze another ride out of the last scrap of daylight. Besides, if I were deliberate enough about the pace I had set, it would be dusk before I set up camp. There would be fewer people around to ask questions, and those who did see me might be content to let me hunker down peacefully in the shadows.

I pitched my tent in some tall grass within view of the store and gobbled down two 79 cent hot dogs loaded with sweet, green relish squeezed from plastic packets. The nutritional content was likely slim, and the relish gave me a sugar high. I squirmed and stared at the roof of the tent for hours, listening to vehicles pull into the parking lot. Every so often, I could pick up muffled bits of conversation as locals walked in and out of the sliding glass doors. More than once, headlights invaded my tent from the street and I thought the police were coming to roust me from my place in the weeds.

By morning, a light frost had crusted over my tent and the vacant lot's dirty brown grass. My camp sat on the edge of a housing development that didn't look much different from the place where I grew up. It was a depressing combination of just-built subdivision homes and muddy lots, ready for backhoe operators and contractors to put up more of the same. The crown jewel of this wonder of cultural expression was the 7-11. I headed over to get some coffee.

Chances were good that I'd spend most of the day outdoors, so I filled a Big Gulp cup with steaming brew in hopes of staying warm.

I struck up a conversation with the woman behind the counter, explaining my road home. She was sympathetic but suspicious, and made sure not to lose sight of me while serving one of her regular customers. I overheard the guy mention heading up the Interstate and asked if he had room for one more. He just glanced over at me and left. The clerk did not say anything about it, but it was obvious that line of questioning made her uncomfortable. Attempts to pick up our earlier discussion were strained – I was no longer a guy in for coffee and chat. I was now a drifter.

The store provided cover for a few more minutes before I tried my luck with one more person who came inside. He shook his head with a newspaper in one hand, coffee in the other and walked out. The clerk had had enough.

"You can't hang around here all morning asking people for rides."

"I'm just trying to get home."

"I know that. I hope you get there. But you have to leave the store."

Off I went. There was movement in the lot where I had spent the night. A guy my age was slashing through the waist-high grass. He looked even rougher than I did. I judged his beard to be a ten-day effort. Grime covered the man's baggy, grey clothing, and his hair was a thicket of snarls. He smiled, exposing a gap where there should have been a canine tooth.

"Hey there," he said.

"Hey."

"Which way are you headed?"

"North."

"Uh huh. I'm trying to get to Miami. Waited too long before going south. Now it's too cold for this shit. How long have you been on the road?"

"About six months."

"Where are you coming from?"

"South America."

"Shit. What were you doing down there?"

68

"Riding a bike."

"What happened to it? Did you bust the engine?"

"No, it was a bicycle. It took a beating on those South American roads, so I left it in Brazil."

"Brazil, huh? How'd you get here?"

"I had enough cash for a plane ticket to Miami."

"Right. So how far north are you going?"

"Canada."

"Aw, dude! I am sorry to hear that. I spent six weeks trying to get from Illinois to Florida and it is cold as a mutherfucker up there right now. And you're going to Canada? Man, I hope you've got some warm gear."

"I've got a tent."

"Well, that's better than nothing. Why are you going to Canada, man?"

"I've got some people up there."

"Shit, that is gonna be some cold. What route are you taking?"

I told him about thumbing west through the South and swinging north in California.

"Dude, California is not giving rides. I was there last summer and nobody picked me up. I went days without a ride. Are you sure you wanna do that?"

Not getting rides was something I didn't want to think about.

"I guess I'll have to take my chances."

"I suppose so. You got a smoke, man?"

"No. Sorry man."

"No sweat. Look man, be careful on that highway. There are some crazy bastards out there and they ain't playing around."

The fear in his eyes was unmistakeable. An old-school road campaigner, he had to have taken some terrifying rides – probably lots of them. I would have liked to hang around to swap some tales and maybe get an idea of what had kept him alive this long, but we both had places to go.

"Yeah, you watch out yourself, man. South Florida is no picnic."

We exchanged the faintest of smiles and parted ways. I had put only a few steps behind me when a new Hyundai pulled toward the gas tanks at the 7-11. The driver was a college kid – a good candidate for a ride, but stealth would have to be the order of the moment. Having just been tossed out of the store, I would have to wait until he'd gassed up and was ready to go. That might leave just enough time to make my pitch before the clerk caught on.

It worked, and it was a great ride, too. The guy's folks had just bought him a brand new car for tooling around campus. The seats were stacked with firm cushions, the heater blasted from multiple directions and more than a hint of new car smell remained. He was heading north to Lake City to visit his parents – a long drive that would terminate close to Interstate 10. Things were looking up. The student had never picked up a hitchhiker before. He said he thought he never would, but my approach at the gas pump made it seem less like hitchhiking and more like a guy just asking for a ride.

I talked about my travels to make conversation; he parroted some aphorisms collected from political science textbooks. It was all right for the first 10 minutes, but my lack of proper bathing began to work its way into the ride as the main, albeit unspoken, topic. The initial clue I was stinking the car out came from the pitch in the driver's voice. He spoke in progressively deeper tones and I couldn't figure out why. It sounded as though he had developed a head cold on the spot. Then I understood that he was breathing through his mouth so he wouldn't have to smell his passenger. That was regrettable, but I felt no shame – life on the road doesn't come with free cologne. Still, as the two-hour drive neared the midway point, I began to appreciate the gravity of my own stink. I thought for a moment about mentioning it but scrapped the idea – what good could come of that? Time dragged. At last, we reached Lake City.

We'd stopped near a gas station and as the college kid drove out of sight, I noticed the cold. North Florida was absolutely biting. I began to shiver. But it was just noon, leaving plenty of time to figure out the next move. I tried my luck again with people filling their tanks rather than walking back to the highway.

The first person I approached told me to get lost. The next guy I asked growled and swore at me. A convoy of families pulled in after that. I assumed asking the minivan set for a lift would be pointless, so I stayed out of their way, all the while becoming more intensely aware of the bracing cold. I hopped from one foot to the other. My fingertips numbed and I rubbed my hands together and blew on them.

A candidate drove up in an early '80s Chrysler. I steeled myself to make a solid delivery, but my voice caught in the chill and I stuttered.

"I gave all my spare change to the last guy who asked."

"No, no. I don't want money; I'm trying to get to Canada."

"Oh, bullshit. Get away from me before I call the cops."

I had never stooped to begging before and I wasn't doing it now. But this guy had made me for a bum and I was furious. His insolent expression made it clear he knew how angry he had made me.

"You got something else to say, man?"

Who was I kidding? A few short days of nearly cash-free travel had turned me into a bum.

"No," I spat. "You have a nice day."

"Hey, you too, ass-face."

I spun on my heels and stomped toward the road. It was measly consolation that being so hopping mad made me briefly less aware of the cold. My patch of ground next to the Interstate offered a particularly bleak vantage point. Cars zoomed by. None so much as slowed down. Freezing, I considered my position: I'd managed to spend more than half of the 75 dollars in my possession when I arrived in Miami and, despite hitching for four days, I was still in Florida. The temperature kept dropping, and I needed a shower in the worst way. I wanted to cry. Instead, I stood still for three hours, eyes watering as I squinted into the headwind. I no longer saw passing cars but an amorphous blur.

I snapped to attention when my ears perked at a frequency they hadn't heard all afternoon – a human voice.

"Hey, where are you going?"

I was too stunned to answer. I just stared at a guy who had come up from behind me.

"Do you want a ride?"

I mumbled that, yes, I did. A small Toyota truck sat idling on the gravel shoulder.

"You can put your gear in the back."

I could hardly believe I was about to get out of the cold. I tore open the door and the heat felt like a roaring fireplace. It was the greatest relief ever.

"Cold day to be doing what you're doing. I'm James Tosca. What's your name?"

I introduced myself and thanked him for pulling over.

"No trouble at all, really. I'm an ex-Air Force man. I was stationed in Southeast Asia for years and any time I got leave I'd thumb all over the place. I was able to see most of Thailand and the Philippines because people picked me up. So now I pick up hitchhikers all the time – kinda paying back, y'know?"

"Well, I sure appreciate it."

"Yeah, no problem. So how far are you going?"

He smiled when I told him.

"That's a long way. But this could be the best ride of your travels so far. I'm driving to Amarillo, Texas. That's about 1,200 miles from here. You can ride with me the whole way if you want."

I told him that sounded great. But it would take time for the offer to sink in. A single ride all the way to Texas? I needed more information, but that could wait. I was enjoying the truck's heater too much to ponder the guy's angle.

Despite exhaustion, I found myself having to chitchat. Fair enough: James had been alone on the road for a long stretch and wanted some company. Only in his late 40s, he was recently retired and still looked the military part. James had close-cropped salt-and-pepper hair, a neatly trimmed moustache and a toned physique. As it happened, he wasn't completely out of touch with the Air Force.

"I'm on my way to the base at Panama City for a two-day seminar. They're testing some new flight safety stuff. I've got a contract to assess and pick which brand the Air Force goes with. It's not a bad way to make a paycheque."

I had spent several days in the Panamanian capital months before and wondered what the hell he was talking about.

"Panama City? Isn't that a fair bit south of here?"

"No, no. Lots of people wonder about that when I first mention it. It's the Tyndall Air Force base and it's in the Florida panhandle. They've set me up with a hotel room there. You're more than welcome to sleep on the floor if you want. I'm not supposed to have any guests but I've stayed enough times and no one ever checks. I'm there for a couple of days before heading to Dallas to pick up my brother and drive him to Amarillo."

I nodded wearily. Why was this guy so eager to help me out? His story of wanting to return the favour for years of his own hitchhiking became less plausible with each additional offer of kindness. James hadn't mentioned his marital status but wore no wedding ring. Was he another highway cruiser looking for action from desperate men trying to get out of the cold? He didn't give off that sort of vibe, but I'd have to keep my guard up. I stared at the purpling western sky. Meantime, James concentrated on more than just traffic; he pulled over in front of a man clomping alongside the Interstate.

The guy had no idea we'd stopped. James hollered three times before he even looked up. As the man neared the truck, I made out his frozen, stoned expression. The lowest part of me took petty satisfaction that his presentation was far worse than mine was. He had on a filthy, moth-eaten sweater over top of untold layers of shirts. His jeans were torn wide open at the thighs and his tattered shoes didn't look like they would survive another step. The man had slung a ripped garbage bag across one shoulder and a long red beard blew over the other one.

The moment of self-satisfaction turned to pity and then to worry – maybe only a few short ticks on the clock would pass before I looked like this guy, was this guy. The dude had to be out of cash. I'd been humbled a few times in South America, but I had had the money to retreat to a hotel and dust myself off. Holding a wee stash of bills afforded me the indulgence of remaining isolated and free, ridiculously viewing myself as some sort of existential outrider. During my travels, I had seen hundreds of destitute, forgotten souls, and now, with accounts dwindling, I could only think that I would soon join them as detritus on the highway.

I couldn't avoid the man's wasted eyes. He was high on something powerful – an effective method for dealing with the cold. The wayfarer made no complaint or any other intelligible sounds; this guy had checked out. Walking was all he could muster. James was eager to help him.

"Where are you going?"

The walker only stared.

"Do you want a ride? I'm driving to Panama City. I can give you a lift."

Nothing.

"Hey, look I'm not trying to harass you here. I'm just saying that if you want you can jump in the back and I'll take you up the Interstate a ways. Where are you trying to get to?"

"Uhhh...."

James saw he might be getting through.

"How far are you going?"

"Pensacola."

We weren't going that far that day. The turnoff to Panama City was 90 miles ahead, where we would head south at Highway 231. That left another 90 miles from the junction to Pensacola – one hell of a long walk. Still, if the guy could manage to get himself into the back of the pickup, it would save him lots of cold trudging time. At last, he carefully lifted his split-open garbage bag, murmured thanks and hopped in the back.

It all made me believe James was telling the truth about returning good deeds for the rides he had taken in Asia.

"Boy, that guy is sure out of it," James said.

"Yeah, I'd say about equal parts frozen and stoned."

"You're probably right. At least he'll get a little closer to Pensacola."

But the poor bastard was still freezing in the back. The harsh truth of the truck's compact space made me overjoyed that being first ensured a spot in the cab. Later, James dropped off the walker and we drove toward the base. He said I could have the first shower once we'd checked in, but I decided on a bath instead. Hot, steaming water gushed out of the tap; as the basin filled, I could feel sweat and grit from two continents washing away. I began to shiver again, and my shoulders ached with the thaw. James knocked at the door.

"Hey, you've been in there for an hour. Can I get in soon?"

An hour? Damn, it couldn't have been. I was still warming up.

"Yeah, I'll just be a minute."

"There's a robe in the closet that you can use, and there's a washing machine down the hallway if you want to do a load of laundry," James told me.

Luxuriating in the freshly pressed robe, I discovered that the laundry machines were free, but a box of Tide cost 75 cents. A sign next to the detergent instructed patrons to deposit quarters into a cardboard box. My lack of change would not deprive me of clean underwear. I unloaded my sorry collection of rags into the washing machine and dumped in stolen soap. Everything was soaked. Garments from the bottom of the pannier smelled of mould. I clicked on the washer and listened to the hiss of hot water pouring over my clothes.

Back at the room, James had thrown some blankets onto the couch. I made them into a bed and dozed off. It was morning when I heard James moving about the room.

"Hey. Hey, are you awake?"

Sunlight poured through the windows. I was sleepy and more comfortable than I'd been in weeks.

"Yeah," I replied with a croaky morning voice.

"I've got an oh-eight-hundred appointment with some brass. You can stay here if you want. I'll be back around fifteen-hundred. There's coffee on, and some leftover pizza on the table."

"Thanks."

I wanted to go back to sleep, but growls erupted from my belly. The coffee smelled good. I rose and grabbed a cup, considering it a marvellous thing not to have to count a handful of change to see if I could afford some. Three slices of pepperoni pizza remained and I sat, chomping on them, watching daytime TV. A rerun of "The Price is Right" came on and the sight of a white-haired Bob Barker shilling retail prizes filled me with delight. I loved to watch that show when I was a kid, and seeing it then was comforting. My clothes were still in the machine, spun out and stuck to the sides. I had just put them in the dryer when the phone rang.

"Hey, did you see the keys to my truck?" James asked. "They're on the counter."

"Yes, I see them."

"You can borrow the truck if you want to go for a boot."

The last thing I wanted to do was leave the room. A loathsome feeling had begun to nag about just what the hell I was going to do after this gravy train pulled out of the station. Outside the hotel room, the morning sun illuminated a world that was cold, terrifying and lethal. I was more than happy to leave the curtains drawn for the time being.

"No thanks, I'm fine just watching TV."

"Okay. I just wanted you to know that they're there if you need them for anything."

James phoned repeatedly throughout the day, his tone and line of questioning taking a turn. It sounded like he was trying to guess how long it would be before I stole his truck. This didn't jibe. What was going through his head? Military paranoia? Maybe he was setting me up. Either way, the about-face put me on the defensive. When he returned later that afternoon, he glanced around the room, as though searching for any sign I had done something criminal.

"Supper's on at the mess hall at seventeen-hundred. Do you want to come along?"

"Yeah, sounds good…. Um, are there any dinner specials tonight?"

"I don't know about that. All I pay as a guest is five bucks – it should be the same price for you."

We left the hotel at quarter-to-five, the early evening wind nipping at my face. I had been continuously warm for almost twenty-four hours – a good feeling. The walk across the compound was enjoyable because I was dry and my clothes were clean. It was also my first good look at the place: a sprawling complex of low-rise buildings and runways. Jeeps buzzed and aircraft criss-crossed the sky. A sense of amazement stuck with me that I was able to walk among all this military hardware without anybody stopping to ask me, "Who goes there?" or "What's the password?" We had cleared most of the base before I saw uniformed men and a few women filing into a drab, single-storey building next to a chainlink fence. James threw open the door and the aroma of roast beef and gravy steamed through the air.

My mouth watered when I saw the Air Force people sitting down at the long rows of tables to heaps of mashed potatoes and gravy with juicy slices of meat. No decent meal had passed my lips since before landing in Miami. Hurrying to a seat, I nearly tripped over a table leg and sent my food to the floor. Then I tore into the beef with feral abandon, gobbling the boiled peas and carrots, and slurping at the gravy. I had nearly cleared my plate before James finished yakking with someone in a uniform. A half-smile crossed his face as he sat down with his tray.

"They sure make good food here, don't they?"

I had to clear my throat of not-yet-downed potatoes before I could respond.

"Yeah, it's amazing."

"The man I was talking to over there is a Major. He organized the flight-gear demonstration tomorrow for me and the fly-guys. I asked him if you could sit in. He says it's no problem if you want to come. What do you think?"

The offer sounded more like an order. I couldn't help wondering if James merely wanted to keep an eye on me, though I still didn't know why. Then it dawned on me he might be trying to give me a taste of military life to convert me. There was no chance I'd ever join up, but I agreed to attend the class for the sake of keeping the peace. Besides, if we were going to fly somewhere, I was all for it.

"Yeah, that'd be cool. I've never been on an Air Force plane."

"No, you've got the wrong idea. We'll be in a lecture hall with an overhead projector. But you should still come. You might learn something."

It seemed unlikely I would learn anything useful.

"You'll need to be up at oh-six-hundred tomorrow morning."

"No problem," I said, wanting to get back to my roast beef.

The alarm clock tore me out of a deep slumber. James' noisy march about the room set the tone for the morning.

"Hey, c'mon. Let's get going. We've got to be done breakfast by oh-seven-hundred hours."

Within minutes, we were trudging once again toward the mess hall. Two quick cups of coffee helped cut through my grogginess. In the lecture room, an urn had been brewing long enough to fill the place with the smell of morning. I grabbed yet another cup and sat down. Thirty young airmen sat on the benches at the back of the room. Five or six of them eyed me up.

At exactly 7:30, James closed the door and outlined the day. He introduced me as a hitchhiker before getting into his spiel. The military men greeted me with unwelcoming grunts. None of them looked as though they were looking forward to the seminar either. I girded myself for a long day as James kicked off his pitch. I couldn't pay atten-

78

tion to him, now zipped on a heavy dose of caffeine, and drifting back through fragments of the past six months. Some of it was a drunken blur. Other moments burned in my brain like a neon branding iron.

Excuse me Mr., can't you see the children dying? – BEN HARPER

Long before I got to Colombia, the locals had warned me not to go out after dark. I began to understand the dangers after meeting up with Machine Gun Manuel that night in Honduras. But the brazen robbery in El Salvador proved that the time of day had little to do with when things were safe. Still desiring all the cracked mystery and madness that lay ahead, I rode hard over broken highways and ate in the cantinas of impoverished Central American towns. Looking on the grinding existence of the inhabitants of those forgotten backwaters became an exercise in detached anguish. The sight of a young woman, back burdened by a mini-haystack of laundry, and four or five dirty, barefoot children at her feet was normal. The harshness of the shantytowns with their contaminated drinking water and scant medical care also checked out as 'normal.' These things shocked me, but I took some comfort that the people bore their load with stoic dignity.

One morning a woman and her children accosted me after I had finished breakfast in a grubby Honduran village. They must have seen me retrieve my bike from behind the restaurant, dashing after me before I could roll out on the highway. I didn't even hear them until a strong, sinewy hand grasped me by the upper arm, spinning me around in surprise. The woman couldn't have been any more than 25.

But the deep fissures in her face told a story of many more years – even decades. She looked furtively over each shoulder before pleading in Spanish, holding out her hand as she motioned toward the young ones. The look in her dark brown eyes was frantic.

The youngest child, a girl, was barely old enough to walk. She wore a stained tee shirt with a silkscreen of a motorcycle rider on it. The shirt was far too large for her, and had been sewn into a sort of a pullover dress. Her blackened feet had sores on them. I doubted whether she'd ever worn shoes. Her two older sisters, I guessed ages four and five, had on badly stitched dresses with pink and yellow flower prints on them. The eldest daughter had outgrown her garment; the hemline looking much higher than was intended. Two boys, the oldest being no more than eight, wore jeans. Only the biggest boy had a shirt. He was also the only one in the family with any footwear – a pair of flip-flops. All of them looked malnourished; all stared at me without saying a word. Their mother, also in ill-fitting, filthy attire revealed a slight bump in her midsection; another was on the way.

Their wretchedness was too much to bear. I'd given money to an impossibly small fraction of the masses reduced to begging in Latin America. But that morning came as a revelation: I had gotten used to seeing people looking for charity at border crossings and in big cities, not in towns as small as that one. I had figured a tacit order reigned in such places, and begging wasn't part of it. The village looked as though it might receive four visitors in a good year, so how could begging work as a sustainable enterprise? Maybe the rarity of targets fired the woman's resolve to cash in. She hissed and jabbed her hand forward again to hurry me up, her eyes darting in terror.

I pulled out all the bills that remained after I'd paid for my breakfast. The woman snatched them up and was gone, cutting a fathomless impression in the bargain. She had none of the look of the professional beggar so common in the big cities; a destitute confidence tends to mark those hustlers. This woman's expression of absolute fear shook me, yet I could only guess why she was afraid. Maybe she was trying to circumvent a beggar's hierarchy or fool a dangerous husband. I nearly got sick imagining what violence awaited the woman if anyone knew she had a little money.

Prying into the stark mode of survival in Central America was turning into a bad idea. Only my own idiocy kept me going. I still don't know what I expected while daydreaming about these travels back home, but this wasn't it. I saw nobody in those countries having an easy time. It got so that I dreaded riding further south for fear of colliding with people in even more hopeless straits. For lack of a better idea, I pedalled onward to the Nicaraguan capital of Managua as fast as I could, stopping only for meals and sleep.

It got hotter as the ground flattened out beyond the border. Broad-leafed palms grew beside the road and traffic was thin, helping me to make out the constant tittering of jungle birds. I spotted parakeets, distinguishing their bright green plumage from the flourishing jungle cover. I even saw hummingbirds, and heard what I thought must have been monkeys in the woods. Three humid days later, I arrived in Managua, fatigued and thirsty, and having picked up a stinging fungal infection on the inside of my right leg. I found a discount backpacker joint across from a general store that sold cervezas. After a couple of days of lazing and drinking, I was ready to check out the town.

For a capital city, Managua sported an abnormal look. It spread in all directions with no centre – some parts of it alive with people, some almost empty. Devastating earthquakes had rocked the city in 1931 and 1972; the old downtown was eventually abandoned because of fault lines beneath. Clusters of decrepit buildings remained in the barrio, deserted except for squatters. I should say I never saw anyone squatting there, but the network of laundry lines strung between condemned buildings and the smell of cooking fires rising from them marked them as inhabited. Edifices from the 1930s still stood, their cement walls cracked, sweeping balconies jutting over the streets. Graffiti images of the communist hammer and sickle remained in faded spray paint throughout the neighbourhood, having survived the Sandinista/Contra war. None of the buildings had windows in them and the whole vicinity was unnaturally still.

I explored the area with a Danish guy named Troels I'd met at the hostel. He had wild auburn hair, a bushy beard and a quick temper. I couldn't pronounce his name properly, which agitated him. He also got a little piqued when I raised the topic of the civil war.

"This has been over for five years and I do not care about it – and I am certain the people here only want to leave it in the past! Let us just check out this quarter like adventurers with no idea about the history."

We explored the ruined municipal cathedral, now covered in pigeon poop; an armed guard was appointed to its care for some reason. A patch of corn grew next to a derelict house and two piglets squealed across the street, their owners nowhere in sight. Four blocks away sat hovels built out of junk, but there were no people. Other than the guard, we saw only five locals scuttling about. It had the feel of the main street of a small town in a cowboy movie, just before the gunfighters trot up to the saloon.

As we headed toward a market in one of the busier areas, a sound came from beneath us.

"Meow!"

Troels and I stopped and looked at each other.

"Meow!"

"This is a cat we are hearing. He must be in the sewers. I think we should try to get him out."

Ten feet from us, a coverless manhole gaped in the road – a common feature in Latin America. I'd never asked anyone about it, but guessed that the heavy metal lids must be worth money, causing their regular disappearance. It made riding in the cities a dangerous undertaking: Open chasms twice nearly swallowed my bicycle. The kitty must have met the same fate.

"Yeah," I said. "Have you got your flashlight?"

84

"Yes. It is always in my side pack. This will help to find the cat."

"If you wanna climb down there I'll hold the light from up here."

"No. I think that because I have come prepared with the torch that it should be your job to get the cat out of the hole."

"I'm not going into the sewer, Trolls."

"My name is Troels! Please try to get this correct. Let us be sensible about this. We cannot leave the pussy cat in the drain pipe."

Troels had a point. The kitty cat was in trouble and we had to hurry.

"How 'bout rock, paper, scissors?"

"Excuse me?"

"Yeah, it's a game used to make decisions."

"This is no time for games."

"No, no. It'll just take a second and it will make the decision for us to see who goes in to get the cat."

"Meow! Meow!"

"I don't like this idea. But the cat should be out. Okay, how do you play?"

I explained what the hand motions represented. I thought it odd such a thing was unheard of in Denmark.

"On three, then," I said.

"Aha! I have a rock to crush your paper," Troels declared.

"No, man. The paper wins on that one – paper beats rock, rock beats scissors, scissors beats paper."

"This is not what you said before the game. How can a piece of paper beat a rock? I believe you are trying to cheat me," said Troels, his voice flaring.

"Aw, come on man. You know I said paper beats rock."

"You certainly did not."

"Meow!"

"All right," I said, exasperated. "Gimme the damn flashlight."

Troels pressed it into my palm and I shone a beam down the hole. The drop looked about five feet, but there was water at the bottom –

raw sewage I guessed by the smell. The cat shimmied out of sight and its cries faded. The two of us looked down the road and saw another manhole – this one had a cover on it. When I yanked it off and angled the light to the left, the meowing grew louder. A tiny, black shape came into view. It wasn't a cat; it was a kitten. The critter looked right up at me and meowed for all its little lungs were worth.

"Here, Troll, hold the flashlight for a second."

"It's Troels!" he said angrily, snatching the light.

He aimed it downward as I lowered myself into the sewer. I could see that the water rose only as high as the kitten's leg joints. My feet splashed in the putrid stream and the kitty scurried over to me. I bent over and pinched it at the scruff of the neck, lifting the little feline to the surface.

"Meow! Meow!"

Troels caught the moment on his super-deluxe, European mega-lens camera. Grinning, he grabbed my camera and snapped a shot for me as well.

"This is very good. We have saved the pussy cat and now we have pictures as well."

"I think I saved the pussy cat, Trolls."

"No, it was my light that made the rescue possible. And I would have gone if I had lost the paper and rock game. This is an even mission."

"Okay, fine. Do you want to take the cat?"

"No, I do not. Look at how dirty he is. I would say that we should let him go. Unless you can think of something better."

I wasn't about to take this surely disease-ridden kitten anywhere. I didn't feel good about it, but I placed the little cat on the pavement and told it to stay away from manholes. The kitten didn't move, but at least it had stopped mewling. Troels and I walked off toward the market.

I wanted to move on the next day, but the fungal infection on my leg had reddened, spreading painfully toward my crotch. A failed two-block trial ride convinced me to seek pharmaceutical treatment and pack my bike onto a bus. But I now had a travel partner; Troels climbed on the same transport, heading to Granada. We found our way to a dockside ticket booth just outside of town later that afternoon, and I was figuring out passage across Lake Nicaragua, when a wine bottle shattered inches from my feet. Startled, I turned to find the thrower: a guy about 20-years-old, high on inhalants. In the cities farther north, I had seen lots of people sniffing glue and gasoline. This guy had the same jerky, watery eyes. The pigmentation in his irises had also faded to an unnerving pallor.

He yelled at me through a mouthful of filthy slobber. Two sailors who were already running up the dock grabbed him, threw him to the ground and laid into him with vicious kicks. I shouted for them to stop, but they kept going until an older man in an oil-stained cap put his hands on their shoulders. The new arrival convinced them to quit it, but by then the glue-sniffer was bleeding and had broken bones.

The peacemaker turned out to be the captain of the boat Troels and I would board. His face was a grid of wrinkles and he had meaty hands with grotty fingernails. The skipper stood out from the locals with his blue eyes and shocks of blond hair stringing down from under his cap. I had mistaken his boat for a tug. The thing looked like a tugboat, with its minimal deck space and upturned bow, but it soon filled with riders crossing Lake Nicaragua. The lake is the biggest one in Central America, stretching just over 100 miles from north to south, and home to rare species of freshwater sharks and sawfish. We cast off and the shoreline soon blurred into a mishmash of greens. Hours later the island of Ometepe with its twin volcanoes rose out of the water.

The captain moored briefly at the town of Altagracia, but I had set my sights on more remote ports. I had heard it was possible to enter Costa Rica from a river that ran off the lake. Troels had been animated about the prospect of setting foot on a volcanic island and hoped I'd change my mind about the longer trip once I saw the place. To my surprise, he said he'd give Ometepe a miss as well, that he'd hop the riverboat to Costa Rica with me. I had hoped to go alone, but decided I could live with the company. We spent two nights drinking beer in a tiny jungle settlement on the Nicaraguan side before setting sail.

Boating into Costa Rica was spectacular. The river looked like a sequence from an old episode of "Wild Kingdom." Copses of balsa and ebony trees blended with vines and brilliant flashes of flowers. Steam rose from the riverbanks and the smell reminded me of greenhouse shops back home. Howler monkeys swung from the treetops, roaring. Smaller primates sprang from vine to branch, looking down at the boat and shrieking. Scarlet macaws, toucans and a kaleidoscope of other birds flew overhead or perched in trees. Turtles swam or dried off on logs and Troels kept saying, "This is so excellent! This is so excellent!" The only disappointment was not seeing any crocodiles.

Erupting Volcano Arenal and its hot springs summoned us next. Troels and I spent an afternoon lounging in a scalding pool, watching the tiny Jesus Christ lizards run across the water. We got out and trudged the three-mile road to the volcano as heavy rain began to pelt. Troels irked a four-foot-long snake along the way, nearly stepping on it. The thing reared up and hissed like a cobra. I couldn't stop laughing as it slithered off. Troels looked like he was going to have a heart attack.

The Dane had settled down by the time we got to Arenal. The volcano was calm, too – nothing was happening. Other travellers had begun to congregate. Word was the stack continually spewed lava that was only visible at night. A murmur of doubt spread among the assembled gringos; hadn't most of us seen pictures of lava taken in the daytime? It sounded like a joke the locals liked to play on dimwitted foreigners. But as darkness fell, the rumours proved true. Luminous splotches of molten rock radiated against the blackness. A matrix of lava ropes glowed into the night. Gasps burst from the crowd of people who had lately poured out of a tour bus. Cameras clicked and flashed, but predictably inside of half-an-hour, tourists' feet were shuffling impatiently and it was time to go.

Troels and I parted ways a few days later, and I ended up on a beach, watching some guys play soccer. Long-haired Ticos booted the ball with bare feet, gracefully manoeuvring across the sand and dazzling with full-flight overhead kicks. They let me sub in when someone left the game, but my tenure as a mid-fielder was short-lived. Charging across the beach to challenge for a loose ball, I stopped short and crumpled to the ground in pain. The hot sand had acted like an emery board, filing off layers of skin. Limping from the field, I discovered the soles of both feet were bleeding.

That much further from being in riding shape, I boarded a bus to Panama City with 50 overly cheerful, hymn-singing Evangelicals from Lubbock, Texas. They were off to a revival meeting in the Panamanian capital and came equipped with religious pamphlets for my reading enjoyment. One guy in the seat in front kept turning around to quote bits of scripture as he thought they related to travel in Central America. I did not see the connection and told him as much. Still, I didn't want to come across as uppity, so I joined in when they all sang "Amazing Grace." It was the only hymn I knew, and I'd be lying if I said I didn't enjoy temporarily belonging to the group.

My new travel partner was making the trip through Central America's southernmost country less amusing. In an unfortunate bit of horse-trading, I succeeded in swapping Troels for a remarkably irritating Scotsman. He materialized like a louse from the Lubbock congregation. I initially thought he was one of them until he made sure to grab the seat next to me.

"Hello there. I knew ya weren't wi' this crowd by the look o' ya. I'm tryin' ta get ta Colombia. I thought maybe we could go together. Yer goin' tha' way too, aren't ya?"

"I might be heading that way – eventually. I thought I'd hang around the Canal to see if I could catch a lift on one of the boats heading further out, to Suriname."

I'd had Suriname on my mind for years. It was a little known out-post with lots of still unexplored jungle. I'd get there if I could.

"Tha' sounds like fun too! Hell, I'll come along tha' way wi' ya if our ship comes in, as they say."

Being stuck inside the rolling church was annoying enough; I didn't need another tag-along. In hopes of changing the subject, I introduced myself and extended my hand. The Scot was reluctant about the formality

"I'm Chet. They call me Chet Two Fingers 'cause I've only go' two fingers on my right hand."

Not knowing what to do with the awkward moment, I asked him how he lost the digits.

"I'll tell ya aboot it sometime – maybe on our way to Suriname or Colombia," he said anxiously.

Before I could explain that I'd soon be back on my bike, the Texas Christians cranked out another spiritual. Chet didn't wait for a second when they stopped.

"I'm sure we could get a boat bound for either o' those places. Shit, this is tha Panama Canal we're talkin' aboot!"

"Look Chet, I'm travelling by bike. My ride is stowed in the bag-gage compartment underneath the bus. I – "

"Yeah, yeah, I saw ya puttin' the thing on. Looks pretty beat up. Maybe now's tha time ta unload it. Ya might be able ta get it onto an ocean liner sailin' ta Colombia. Bu' you'll never get it there if ya have ta fly, and if ya end up goin' to Suriname you'll probably have ta take a freighter and they'll never le' ya stow it. And for sure you'll no' be able ta ride through tha Darien Gap."

Chet was on to something there. The Pan-American Highway stretched into Southern Panama, but stopped short of the Colombian line before picking up again in South America. Darien's jungle was impenetrable. Riverboats wound through the gap, though the scuttle-butt was that drug traffickers and Colombian guerrillas controlled most of them. Rumours of killings had drifted out of Darien and I had planned to find another way south. Chet babbled on about where I might end up and how I might get there, pestering me to travel with him instead. He was in his mid-40s – older than most other travellers I'd run across. The washed-up backpacker rambled into a weird diatribe that made me think he had taken too many party favours back in the '70s.

"So, as I was travellin' through Northern Nigeria, I thought ta myself, y'know, bein' a two-fingered onanist is no picnic. Then I got ta thinkin' tha' I really should phone home more often. Right away, I told the mufti tha' I needed ta use a phone. Well, as I found oot, there aren't many phones in Hausa territory, so I had ta hire a jeep tha' would take me ta the nearest town tha' had one. As I'm sure ya can imagine, tha' was a dusty trip! Man alive! We drove for two days and wouldn't ya know it – the phone was bust. Well, no' only would my aunties be disappointed but I'd no' find oot how the Glasgow Rangers had fared...."

Wholeheartedly wishing the choir would strike up again, I feigned sleep until the other riders exclaimed that we were approaching the Bridge of the Americas. The vast arc spanned the Panama Canal and linked two continents. Enough daylight remained to illuminate the single freighter plying the waterway. Thirty minutes later, we pulled into the Panama City bus depot. Chet invited himself to share a hotel room with me, suggesting we share a bed, "I'm no' a homose'shual, it'll just be cheaper tha' way." We settled on individual bunks and headed out for supper, finding an old Chinese restaurant on one of the docks. Heaping plates of chicken chow mein and chop suey steamed from our plates.

"I tell ya, these Chinese'll go just about everywhere. I've travelled the world and seen 'em on every continent I've been ta – even in Africa. Hell, I had Chinese food in Northern Finland! I know why they leave China – I've been there and it's a hard life."

Chet's burbling chatter ebbed into the din of the restaurant. Swigging my third beer and breathing in the ambience, I felt comfortable in the seediness of the place. Hot, badly lit and smelling of kitchen grease, a dingy intimacy crowded the air. Drunken sailors shouted over each other at the next table. The woman who ran the place yelled dinner orders to the cook in Chinese-accented Spanish and a bedraggled waitress scurried between tables with plates of food and dirty dishes. Overhead pipes hissed and gurgled, dripping into a pool of water in the middle of the floor. Decades on the waterfront had warped all of the wooden furniture into curlicues.

The front door banged open and another gang of tattooed sailors barged in, hollering in an Eastern European tongue. The proprietor eyed them up warily before sending the waitress over to take their orders. A couple of tough-looking guys in suits and fedoras at the back of the restaurant checked out the place, but I doubted they were there for the atmosphere. They had to be waiting for somebody. Both of their heads turned when the door opened again and a hooker in a curly red wig and high heels walked in. They turned away when the restaurant owner chased her out.

The prostitute must have followed the sailors into the restaurant. Or maybe it was part of her dockside circuit. I reflected that most of the Latin American women who had made an impression on me had done so because of their desperation. The poorest women seemed unafraid to get close. It was almost always to beg, and I thought of the courage that must have required. Having been so near to those women engraved in my memory the lines on their faces, the fear and anger in their eyes and the cries of their children. There had been many male beggars, but interactions with them were more like mundane, man-to-man exchanges with no more significance than a handshake or the shared, silent nod across adjacent urinals. Most other men I had ended up in close quarters with were border officials, thieves or soldiers. Those guys had nothing to fear from me. The women didn't either, but they couldn't have known that.

Other than halting conversations with waitresses or female hostel managers, there had been scant interaction with more financially secure women. I couldn't imagine they would have thought there was much to gain by talking anything besides business with me. Being too lazy or too dense to get a handle on the language was also a hindrance, although lots of men – usually in pairs or larger clusters – had stopped to quiz the cycling curiosity laid over in their town. That had to have been part of the reason for the dearth of contact with women: that I was an oddity rambling across the continent, too freakish to approach. I didn't share much common ground with the female travellers I'd met either. A quick chat about recent days on the road or upcoming destinations was the extent of those conversations. Lengthier discussions seemed possible only within a larger group. For a while I scratched my head for being held at arm's length, but it added up when I considered the practicalities: A guy who will ride alone through South America likely had no common sense. Most female travellers were smart enough not to take routes similar to mine. In general, women tended to stay out of the path I'd chosen unless they had no other choice.

Chet jarred me into the present when he began talking sense.

"So I spoke wi' the guy a' tha hotel desk when y'were in tha shower. He says we can ge' a bus ta the Atlantic side o' tha country and take an ocean liner ta Cartagena for cheap. He says there's nothin' o' the sort leaving oot fer Suriname."

"Is that so?"

"I believe the man a' tha hotel gave me the right information. We can check it oot tomorrow, bu' he says the ship costs 90 dollars each if we share a cabin. So it's settled then! Let's take a day or so in Panama and then get ta Colombia. We'll travel all the way down ta Argentina!"

I dodged Chet the day after our ship docked in Cartagena, soon exchanging his inane brogue for sodden chaos in Bogotá. I hoped for an easier time when I left Colombia and crossed the border into Ecuador six weeks later. By then, the skin had grown back on my feet and the infection on my leg had faded. Slowing my torrid drinking tempo also brought relief. But the condition of my bicycle had deteriorated and riding was limited to intermittent spurts.

I pedalled the dilapidated thing along forested roads to the Ecuadorian border post. The lone immigration official eyed my panniers, deliberating whether to search them, but the comfort of his chair won out and he stamped my passport without getting up. Only a short ride followed. My rear wheel crumpled, relegating me to another bus, this time to Quito, nearly 10,000 feet above sea level. Rolling into town just after six o'clock, Quito's energy reminded me of other Latin American hubs. The bus depot bustled with passengers, relatives greeting travellers and porters hefting and wheeling luggage through the station. Bus drivers shouted, "¡Guyaquil! ¡Guyaquil – diez minutos!"

"¡Cuenca! ¡Bus a Cuenca!"

I bumbled along, trying to get my bearings, when I saw a terrible thing. A middle-aged woman crawled across the parking lot on all fours. She could not walk upright and wore shoes on her hands with pads on her knees. No one else gawked as she craned her neck forward to see where she was going. The woman's oversized bottom billowed as she inched toward the street, her belly almost scraping the ground. I looked away, ashamed for having stared.

Shaking off the chill, I set out to find a budget hotel. At a dive called the Belmont, I discovered that the Irishmen I had gotten drunk with at the Platypus were now in Quito. We debauched all over town, even lucking into the opening night for a new club when highballs were free of charge. I spent hungover days wandering the city, appreciative of its cool climate. Quito's old colonial district, neatly split from the modern commercial area, had been declared a world heritage site in 1978. Restored Spanish-settlement-era buildings surrounded the main plaza, and in the mornings, uniformed school children paraded there. Later in the day, members of the local Hare Krishna contingent would caterwaul and solicit donations.

Returning to the hotel was always a pleasure. Cheap as the Belmont was, it had established itself as Quito's gringo hub. The parlour bubbled with activity. One morning during my second cup of coffee, a Japanese couple offered calligraphy lessons, while a table of merry Norwegians chain-smoked and two impossibly geeky Swiss Army deserters pieced together a Barbie jigsaw puzzle. Above the brouhaha, an Australian, a New Zealander and an American plotted a jungle trek. They were happy to take me on as a fourth and we left Quito two days later.

A day of buses, capped with a jouncing ride on the roof of a transport got us to the jungle village of Mishualli on the shore of the Rio Napo. People in the little town were friendly and I could hear the river from my hotel room. We waited there in hopes of lowering the guide-for-hire rate, passing the hours jumping out of trees into the river and watching a band of five monkeys swing branch-to-branch. One particular monkey became my favourite when he stole a Bon Jovi cassette from a guy who had played it incessantly. I cheered as the furry creature scrambled up a tree and reeled out all the tape.

The monkey must have had enough of Bon Jovi as well, and I hypothesized a sort of kindred spirit. Unfortunately, I overestimated the similarity of our worldview. One afternoon the animal hunched on the ground with his back turned to me. Hoping to strengthen our imagined fraternity of monkey business, I stalked the primate from behind with a plan to tickle him. Silent as a jaguar, I advanced within range of the monkey's armpits. I honestly thought he'd find a good tickling in the sensitive armpit area as hilarious as I did. I failed to bridge the monkey/human divide, but I did succeed in freaking him out. He shrieked a piercing "ooooooohh! ooooooohh! ooooooooh!" That turned out to be a simian emergency cry and within seconds the other four monkeys leaped out of the bush, each one attaching to a limb.

I ran, yelping, with monkeys stuck to both arms and legs. My lurching sprint across the square drew the attention of the villagers, who gathered to point and laugh. Flailing and yelling for the beasts to let go, I tripped and squashed one under my weight. It squealed and retreated while the others continued their fight. Still outnumbered three-to-one, I was not out of the battle – far from it. Sensing victory was at hand after freeing myself from the clutches of one monkey, I rose to my feet and twirled the two stuck to my arms like a washing machine agitator, pin-wheeling them this way and then that. At last, they dropped off, reducing the contest to a valiantly fought duel with the tenacious monkey still on my leg. I performed a jig trying to toss the last critter, hopping, twisting and bellowing, "Get the fuck off me, you stupid monkey!" with the little rogue hooting, "EEEEEEE! EEEEEE! OOOOHHH! OOOOOHHHH! EEEEE!" by way of retort. The battle ended at last, as my cycling-strengthened legs managed to fire the beast spinning into the bushes.

Two of my travelling companions had witnessed the skirmish and fell over laughing. I had nothing to say about it; I'd left everything on the battlefield and emerged the clear winner. My new focus was the jungle trek, which got underway the next day and was to last a week. The American in our group, a tall, nerdy guy from Minnesota named Garrett, whined perpetually. The hike was too hard. His feet hurt. There were too many bugs. When was lunch? Not that he didn't have a point – every bug in the jungle sucked blood with gusto and the heat was excruciating. Our progress was slow. Dark green vines sprawled across the forest floor, tripping us up and mud pits lurked, periodically swallowing one or another of us to the knee. I had other problems. The pair of cheap boots I purchased in Quito for the expedition fell apart on the first day. I had to switch to a pair of ill-fitting runners belonging to Stan the Aussie. The shoes cut into my feet and the trudge became an agonizing one.

None of us were used to the jungle. All, except our guide Francisco, had nicks and bruises, and all of us caught a flu-like tropical malady. But Garrett was the only one who complained.

"I'm sorry guys, can one of you carry my pack for a while? It's too heavy for me," he sniffed.

Stan took it without saying anything, but I wondered if he shared the boiling contempt I felt for that guy. My feet were bleeding, and he would have been happy to have me pack his load? However the others felt, we quietly agreed to a rotation of lugging Garrett's bag, the New Zealander, Alex, remarking that the Minnesotan had taken on more than he could handle. Despite Garrett being relieved of his burden, we had to stop and wait for him every time the pathway rose. Alex or Stan would call for him, and we'd judge the length of time we'd be held up by how far away he sounded.

Francisco told us that he had walked this trail less than a month before, clearing it with a machete. Heavy rains in those few weeks had seen the pathway grow over almost completely. Wide-leafed plants with variegated patterns of green sprang up close to the ground, shrubs and purple flowers grew along the pathway and termite-ridden trees had crashed down, further obscuring the trail. Francisco kept in the lead, tirelessly hacking away with his knife at the vegetation that had reclaimed the walkway.

The river flowed close to the trail for part of the hike. On our third day in the jungle, the four of us watched admiringly as our guide used his blade to cut down two balsa trees, quickly fashioning them into a raft. In a whimsical moment, Stan christened it the 'S.S. Muffin' and all of us whooped for joy as Francisco weighed anchor. There was plenty of room for all five adventurers, but we spent most of the day in the pristine water, paddling behind the raft as it drifted and dark shapes of fish swam below. Travelling by river was a relief for all of us, but Garrett could barely contain himself. All day long, he sighed, "Oh, thank God, my feet couldn't take another day of that."

The rest was short-lived, as another day's hike lay ahead before we got to a tiny Huaorani Indian settlement. Seven shacks in a clearing were home to a small clan. Francisco knew them and could speak their language; he secured a bed for himself, while the four of us pitched our tents in the compound. One of our hosts, a squat, muscular man missing his top-front teeth, took pride in demonstrating a blowgun he had made. Eight-feet-long and heavy, it had been fashioned from the wood of a palm tree. The man opened his left hand, revealing three-dozen darts made from a light-coloured wood, wrapped at the base with cotton-like fibres.

The Huaorani craftsman loaded one of the darts into the backend of the tube, aimed at a target 30 feet away, and blew a short gust of air into the gun. The missile struck bull's-eye. Smiling broadly, he passed the gun to me. I fired a dart mere inches from his.

The man laughed and my fellow travellers shouted me down.

"No way – that was a complete fluke!"

"You'll never make another shot like that again."

"Let me try it!"

All of us hit the mark with ease, the long barrel allowing for surprising accuracy. We fooled around with it for a while as our host looked on. Then the man spoke with Francisco and our guide told us that the gun was for sale. None of us bought it and the artisan put it away.

We took to lounging beside our tents and, as the sun was setting, four men trekked out of the jungle. Two of them supported a long wooden spit on their shoulders, dangling a pair of monkeys by their hands and feet.

Garrett was appalled.

"Oh my God! They've killed those monkeys! That's so awful!"

"Don't worry about it, Garrett. That's how people who live in the jungle eat," said Alex.

"But those poor monkeys. The idea of eating them just turns my stomach. Ooohh, God I wish I had a Twinkie."

Stan guffawed in disgust, "Jesus Christ, Garrett! A Twinkie? What planet are you from? Ha ha!"

"Ooohh … Twinkies settle my tummy down."

Bawling squeals issued from the hunting party. One of the men carried a baby monkey. The hunters glanced in our direction and walked to the open fire in the kitchen. Ten minutes later, Francisco brought the tiny creature to our camp. He passed it to Alex, but all four of us wanted in on the action. Stan spoke up.

"Look, the thing's parents have just been killed and probably are being turned into monkey stew right now. Be gentle with the little guy – I'm betting he's really freaked out."

The monkey squeaked and squawked as we took turns stroking its soft, black fur, trying to guess its fate. The mystery ended a few minutes later when somebody marched over from the kitchen and snatched it from us. In just under an hour, we were offered plates of rice and monkey meat. All of us had some except for Garrett.

Monkey meat is chewy and bland, sort of like rubbery liver. Stan was quick to let Garrett know what he was missing.

"Mmmm! A little monkey meat makes me hungry for more," he said, swishing around the boiled, brown flesh on his tongue.

Taking Stan's cue that the crude dinner theatre was payback for Garrett's snivelling, Alex and I grunted and stuck out half-chewed primate on our tongues as well.

"Yeah," I said, "it's about as close to cannibalism as I want to get."

Garrett disappeared inside his tent, nauseated.

I returned to Quito four days later and spent one last drunken night in the city. The Irish crew was still at the hotel, gearing up for Christmas at a legendary backpacker hut known as the Round House. Revered in gringo hangouts all over South America, it apparently sat at the confluence of two rivers near the town of Vilcabamba in Southern Ecuador. The story went that a psychedelic drug, known as San Pedro, was available in large quantities at the tourist office there, and that the coolest cats repaired to the Round House to get high. The Irishmen invited me to join them for a Christmas of peyote-like tripping.

It sounded like a festive time, but holding no ticket home, moving ahead was crucial. I chose a roundabout path back to Canada that entailed crossing a swath of Brazilian jungle. Getting to the Amazon would involve cutting east across Peru, following a bus trip to an Ecuadorian town called Huaquillas. Straddling the Peruvian line, Huaquillas' dusty streets whirred with fringe characters. Cross-border traffic hummed and a high-spirited crowd of moneychangers, beggars and thieves trolled the area for easy targets. An armada of goggle- and scarf-wearing motorcycle cabbies sped every which way, disgorging black exhaust.

Wary after a near collision with one of the cabs, I rolled my bicycle into the immigration office to collect my exit stamp. The guy at the booth told me to leave it outside and I protested, fearing a rip-off. The official smirked as he dragged out the passport stamping into a 15-minute question-and-answer period. I left with the right paperwork, but sometime during the formalities, my panniers had been unzipped and my machete stolen. On the street, a mob of cash traders shouted at me as I wobbled the bike on its now-chronically warped wheels toward the Peruvian entry point. Cursing out loud, I decided to hop a bus to the jungle rather than ride those miles. For the moment, motorized travel was preferable to sweating it out on the mashed-up bicycle. I bought a ticket to Chiclayo on the Peruvian coast, stashed my bike in the lower compartment, and sat down with a bottle of Coke and a book.

Two hours remained before departure, and there wasn't another soul aboard the bus. But I was to enjoy the solitude for only a short time. A garrulous woman got on 10 minutes later, barking at her two children. The kids, a boy and a girl, perhaps five- and six-years-old, ran wild up and down the aisle as their mother loaded their luggage. I successfully tuned out the woman's admonitions to the children, but soon found myself in conversation of sorts.

"¡Gringo!" she said, sharply.

Glancing up from my book, I saw the most unfortunate looking woman I'd ever seen. Afflicted with rolling obesity and cataracts on her eyes, a prominent, dark moustache overshadowed her thin lips. Pockmarks dotted her face and her teeth were brown. As the woman drew uncomfortably close, she disclosed an alarming case of halitosis.

"Ah, ojos azules," she said in a softer, almost breathy voice. I deduced by her gestures that the words meant 'blue eyes.'

"¿Americano?" she asked, reaching out to stroke my hair.

I recoiled as far back into my seat as I could and choked out a "No."

"¿No? ¿Inglés?" she asked, trying again to touch my hair.

"No. Canadiense," I replied, squirming backward.

"¿Canadá?"

"Sí."

Before she could pursue me further, she paused to shriek at her children who were climbing out of a window. I took the opportunity to retreat behind my book, which I held directly in front of my face, effectively shielding me from further advances. As I did so, I wondered what ill-starred bloke she had convinced to perform the sex act with her on at least two occasions. That he was no longer on the scene made perfect sense. When she had finished screaming at her kids, she found me in the defensive attitude I'd assumed with my book.

That didn't stop her from speaking to me in hushed tones and, alternately, in grating ones to her children, who were now spitting chewed-up chocolate bar at one another. I adopted a strategy of hunkering behind my book and answering all her questions with a "sí." Such a tactic, I hoped, would make it clear I was ignoring her. It was the one time when I was actually grateful for my weak language skills.

But the woman would not stop talking. With each "sí" that I uttered, more edge crept into my voice. After half an hour of this silly exchange I proclaimed an especially annoyed-sounding "¡Sí!" and she cried out excitedly, gathered her children and hurried off the bus. I was relieved, but not surprised that the quiet was brief. She returned minutes later with an older woman and a man about my age. They were her mother and brother. The woman, all flustered and jiggling up and down, pointed at me and shouted a flurry of Spanish words, the only one I could understand being "¡matrimonio!"

The woman's mother beamed and walked toward me. Her brother gaped, eyes popping wide. In a frantic attempt to be better understood, I resorted to a juvenile gringo-ese.

"No! ¡No matrimonio! I have wife-o in Canada! ¡No matrimonio!" I yelped, stupidly pointing to a bare ring finger. "I-I left the ring-o in Canada!"

"¡Sí matrimonio! ¡Sí!" the woman shouted and pointed toward a church spire and then at her watch. I took this to mean that she wanted us to conclude a quick wedding service before the bus got going; we could arrive in Chiclayo as husband and wife!

I shook my head vigorously and kept repeating, "Uh-uh, no matrimonio."

A puzzled look crossed her mother's face and her brother broke into a grin. The children had collected handfuls of dirt from outside and were throwing them at each other. The woman rumbled toward me. I could only think that this must not be happening. She stopped at my seat and kneeled, peering directly into my eyes. With a squall of horrid breath, she intoned, "¿No matromonio?"

"No matrimonio," I said with great emphasis.

Her brother slapped his knee, overtaken with laughter. The woman thundered up to him and belted him on the cheek and the two began yelling at each other. Their mother glowered at me, said something to me under her breath and stepped off the bus. The two children, perhaps inspired by their mother and uncle, pulled each other's hair and screamed.

A couple of passengers boarded, sidestepping the squabbling siblings. The bus driver stormed out of the depot at a forced march to see what was going on. The woman and her brother wound down their battle as the driver approached. More people entered and the woman turned her attention to separating her kids, who had lately torn off each other's shirts. With the bus now mobile, the woman and her children lodged themselves in the seat directly in front of me. The ride to Chiclayo took nine hours, my would-be wife turning to fix me with a wrathful stare for the duration.

~

I laughed at the memory of the escape, but James' bloodshot glare told me that I had drifted too far from the Air Force lecture hall. Still, my efforts to focus fell short, and the morning ground along at an excruciating rate. Things did speed up after lunch, however. We were packed and ready to split by three o'clock. James was all business.

"Part of the reason I asked you to ride with me to Amarillo is so we can share the driving. Do you have a licence?"

I had one, but his truck was a standard. My sister had shown me how to drive stick transmission the year before at an empty industrial park. We practiced for an afternoon, but I never attempted it on the street. I told this to James in hopes of begging off the driving.

The Air Force man wasn't easily dissuaded; he drove us to a dirt track off the main road to provide me with a refresher course. Twice, I got us stuck in piles of muck and James swore at me. The lesson made me nervous, especially with James' rancorous flare-ups. The guy shifted seamlessly from baseless suspicion to anger and then to generosity. Sitting through it was like weathering the emotional spectrum of a man corked on whiskey. Whatever his problem was, following an hour of stalls, crunched gears and slaloming apocalyptically through the mud, James pronounced me highway-ready. He took the first shift at the wheel and we were on our way.

At dusk, James decided on Subway sandwiches. We were in Hattiesburg, Mississippi, but we weren't to stay long. Rather than waste time eating at a table, James insisted we take our food on the road. He also announced it was my turn to drive. I swallowed hard. Thoughts of juggling a stick shift, steering wheel and a Subway sandwich with James riding shotgun made me sweat. I left my supper in its wrapper and rested it on the seat, considering it wiser to leave it there until I could grind the transmission into highway gear.

The little Toyota convulsed as I pulled onto the street. James snarled a terse series of commands until we made the highway on-ramp. My shift from third gear to fourth produced a violent jerk. James exploded.

"Balls on a biscuit, man! What the fuck are you doing?"

I wasn't sure.

"I told you ten fucking times – let the goddamned clutch out slowly! We're lucky you didn't stall us on the fucking highway!"

He cursed some more and fired the remnants of his sandwich at the windshield. James had asked for extra mustard and a minor blast radius of it now splattered the glass. He stewed in heavy nose-breathing wrath; I accelerated into a turn. We drove for thirty miles, saying nothing. James attempted nonchalance, using a napkin to remove the coagulating mustard from the windshield. I took a few bites from my sub.

"I'm glad you had a shower."

"What?"

"It was tough when you first jumped into the truck."

"Oh?"

"Yeah, man, you smelled like shit. I had to breathe through my mouth for a while. I let you have the first shower at the hotel so I could sleep that night."

"Well, thanks for not leaving me on the side of the highway."

"No, I wouldn't have done that. I'd just be more careful when thumbing future rides."

I knew the stink thing was a problem, but James' censure underscored its seriousness. Future trucker showers would need to be more frequent. I rolled my eyes in the Toyota's dark cab; my gaminess and his quick temper made for a deranged combination. Despite the pointer, James and his ex-military unpredictability were beginning to piss me off. I perked up a few minutes later when a familiar-sounding broadcast crepitated over the radio. A minor league hockey game was on the air. The play-by-play called in a thick southern drawl surprised me.

"...Addison hits the puuu-uuck to the other ey-end of the rink for an ah-cing cawl."

The announcer's voice contrasted oddly with the sharp, fast-paced commentators I was used to hearing in Canada. The man's relaxed pronunciation loosened my grip on the steering wheel, his cadence slowing the game to an easy tempo.

"...thair's a pass at sayn-ter ahce ... Kapersky picks it uuup aynd carries it into the attackin' zone...."

James had fallen asleep. The hockey game and the repetitive pattern of the night-lit highway lulled me into a reverie.

Y'all got cocaine eyes. – ROLLING STONES

Cocaine held forbidden, exotic allure for throngs of travellers search-ing for the 'Colombian experience.' Hordes of gringos vibrated on the stuff, wired to it. In Cartagena, a young German man I met at a ho-tel told me he had spent his entire six-week vacation free-basing co-caine. His room was littered with empty solvent bottles, a dozen spent lighters, at least that many bent and blackened spoons and hundreds of empty plastic bags. He introduced himself as "Myco." Down the road, I met a Canadian who had also encountered Myco. The travel-ler whistled, giving his head a slow shake: "Is Psycho Myco still in Cartagena? Fuckin' hell – he was getting high in that room when I was there a month ago!"

Psycho Myco told me he paid between two and six dollars a gram for cocaine. He said his "passion" for the drug knew no bounds and that he had smoked 20 grams in one psychosis-ridden session. Psycho Myco's debts racked up. One night a dealer threatened to kill him if he didn't settle the next day. Psycho Myco was still breathing, so I as-sumed he made good.

The German's predicament was unnerving – he said he'd never taken cocaine before arriving in Colombia. His headlong love affair with it had been catastrophic. The guy was emaciated, twitchy and addicted. The fact he'd sunk to free-basing just a few days after trying coke for the first time was a bad sign. Snorting is generally the first rung down into cocaine hell. From there, a user whose honeymoon period has passed will sometimes move into free-basing, which involves mixing flammable compounds with cocaine as part of the process of removing impurities. This is dangerous. People have caught themselves on fire doing it. The end product, assuming there are no fire-related fatalities, is nearly pure cocaine, free of chemical adjunct. When smoked, a user becomes far more stoned than he or she would merely snorting the drug. This degeneration from snorting to free-basing usually takes months, if not years, of regular use. Psycho Myco had proven himself far ahead of that curve. Psycho Myco had also reduced himself to a vision of death.

Psycho Myco was to fly home the day after I met him. I have no idea how he fared back in Germany with a coke addiction to feed. But, farther south, I saw up close the destruction of travellers who had never previously taken anything stronger than beer. In Colombia, cocaine cost about 50 times less than it did on the streets of New York, London or Vancouver. So it seemed like a great deal until addiction kicked in and money flowed out of foreign wallets faster and more steadily than the waters of the Orinoco River. I watched it happen over and over again as I drank myself senseless in Bogotá.

An Australian named Henry, just out of business school, flew to Colombia to learn Spanish. His shipping firm had paid for the excursion, so that he could become fluent and accommodate a booming Spanish-speaking clientele. The first time I saw Henry, he had his nose in a pile of cocaine at the Platypus Hotel. Night had fallen and the samba crowd was gearing up. The hotel had a no-drugs policy, but it was easy for guests to toot wherever they wanted after six o'clock, when most of the staff had gone home. The parlour that was such a congenial place to swill 35-cent-a-bottle Leon beer in the daytime held just as much appeal for cokeheads at night. Henry and a crowd of English travellers snorted and ground their teeth, babbling like madmen.

I sat a few tables down from them, drinking heavily and planning to stay the course far into the evening. The coke party was making noises about heading downtown and I wished they'd hurry up and go. My drinking buddy, an amiable dude from Luxembourg by the name of Raphael, overheard their plan, slammed down his beer and deserted me. He was dating a centrefold babe from the city, and word had it she was the daughter of one of the heaviest drug bosses in Bogotá. I never asked him about it as we knocked back beer – I didn't care. What I did care about was that these stuck-up, coked-out assholes were about to whisk my newfound pal off to some nightclub. I was not invited, my lack of club-cool relegating me to pariah status. I watched as Henry – all six-foot-five of him – put his arm around Raphael and cut him a fat line. Henry shouted a battle cry as Raphael snorted.

I remained a drunken wallflower at the back of the room, plastered to a chair at a table loaded with dozens of empty bottles. The howls from the coke table intensified.

"'Oly fuck! 'Ja see the size 'o that cocksuckin' toot? Look at 'is fuckin' eyes! Ha ha!

"'Ay 'Enry, fix me a toot, yeah?"

"Fuck ya! Let's blast this shit but good. Awright, Pauly – yer turn, have at 'er!"

"Woo-hoo! How's that make ya feel mate? Good enough to make ya wanna get down, I'm hopin'!"

"Too right, man!"

I'd had enough; I staggered to my room and zonked out. Shaking with the after-effects the next morning, I passed Henry in the hall. The big Aussie's nose was caked with blood and I could see he'd been crying. He pretended not to notice me and lumbered to the bathroom. The sight of him was an unpleasant surprise.

It was only ten o'clock, which was early for me to get out of bed. Prematurely running out of people to drink with the night before had put me ahead of schedule. Even though my head felt as though it would split, I took some comfort that I'd had nothing to do with the coke. Any time I'd taken it in the past I felt like killing myself the next day. Things looked like they were shaping up just as badly for Henry. My guess was the rest of his posse would be in sorry condition as well. Flushing sounds came from the bathroom and Henry emerged.

"Fuck, mate. There any coffee on?"

"I think there's some left in kitchen."

"Oh, fuck, fuck, fuck! God, I feel like a ton of mongrel shit. Christ."

Henry trailed off, struggling to choke back a sob. He poured coffee into a cracked mug with a shaky hand, slumping into a chair in the parlour. The empty Leon beer bottles from the previous day were gone and a maid had wiped the table clean. The overhead light was soft and a doorway down the hall opened to the courtyard, admitting the barest hint of a breeze. I didn't know what to do next. There was no one else in the parlour and sitting at a table separate from Henry would surely prove awkward. The Australian only groaned quietly to himself as he grasped his coffee mug with both hands, head down. The fact he had spoken at all made me think I should see if he wanted to talk.

"So it was a rough night, then?"

"Fuck, mate. It's the goddammed nose candy. I get into the shit and I can't let 'er go. I've been in this fuckin' country two months.... Supposed to be learnin' the language. Fuck, mate, I gotta straighten this shit out. Ohhh God...."

Henry lowered his head. A tremor worked itself through his shoulders. He regained control and looked at me.

"Fuck, mate. I never even touched the ganja back home. I mean yeah, I can put back scotches better than most, but that's got fuck all to do with fuckin' coke. This shit's gotta stop."

Henry told me how he'd finished first in business school. His professors built him up, comparing his ideas to those of old-time capitalists like Carnegie or Rockefeller. They said Henry had no need to languish in some backwater apprenticeship, that he was ready to make money. Being eaten alive by cocaine was not something anybody saw coming. Henry worried it would get him fired.

"I can speak a bit of the language, but I've gotta get this together. Fuck, mate, I gotta know this shit when I get back. I gotta break with this crowd and get down to Ecuador. I hear there are towns down there where a gringo can pay a family to take him in and learn it that way."

Henry might find a life preserver with a residential language program. I had considered doing something like that during my stay in Nicaragua. A lack of drive made the decision not to try it an easy one. But my situation was nowhere near as dire as Henry's. A close look at his face revealed a patina of cocaine use and wear, making him appear older than his 25 years. He finished his coffee without saying much else and I switched to alcohol when he left. Somewhere around my sixth beer, Henry stalked back into the room. He still looked terrible, strung out. Even so, his posture was straight up and a faint suggestion of rebirth glowed in his eyes.

"That's it mate! I've booked my bus ticket and I'm heading for Quito first thing. Thanks for yer ear this morning. It was good to get that shit to the light. I'm gettin' gone. Look, there's a thing I've been doing in town here that I feel bad about running out on. How would you like to make some money?"

I cringed. Forging a business connection with a coke addict in Colombia struck me as a bad idea. But I was curious. I took a long pull on my beer.

"What have you got in mind?"

"It's like this. I've got a couple of gigs teaching English to people in the area. One is early in the mornings just having a chat with three guys who work in a pharmacy downtown. The other is a little more serious. I go over some language skills with a class at a local college. That one just ended – problem is I told the headmaster I'd teach the next course, too. But I've gotta get outta here mate. And I'll feel like an asshole if I leave this guy in the lurch. Whaddya say? You wanna teach for cash?"

Half-drunk, I imagined I could pull this off. Not to give the impression that I wanted the work – I didn't. The days of drinking and hatching nebulous plans to get my bike back on the road held far greater charm. Still, it sounded like easy money.

"What does it pay?"

"The morning gig is 25 dollars a week for an hour of teaching, four days a week. The one in the evenings is 35 for an hour, three times a week."

"When do I start?"

"The one at the pharmacy is supposed to go on tomorrow. But I told the boss over there I was leaving. He was slightly pissed. Never mind that, though, I'll patch things up with 'im and tell 'im you're takin' it over. I'll set you up with the headmaster at the university, too."

I finished my brew and reached for another one. Henry and I sat for an hour guzzling beer and going over details. He drank like a man striving not to come apart. Though rattled, Henry took a serious approach to the teaching, irritating me with particulars about lesson plans. I assured him I would get to those in a less-drunken moment, but he insisted on pulling out papers and blithering about class material. The man even droned about ways to take the courses forward. Henry was being a buzz-kill.

I relaxed when he went away. But before he left, Henry gave me three neatly arranged folders, two phone numbers and the assurance he would make the appropriate connections with my future employers. I deposited the paperwork in my room and got into more serious drinking. The next morning, I awoke with a blistering hangover, smelling of rum, unsure about the details of the previous night. Poised to vomit, I heard the phone ringing in the lobby, followed by footsteps and a knock at my door.

"¡Señor! The telephone is for you!"

"Just a minute," I groaned back.

This probably had something to do with Henry's teaching jobs. They now impressed me as a terrible idea. Struggling to find something to put on, I discovered that I was still wearing yesterday's clothes. The only change was that my white, Canadian maple leaf T-shirt now sported a sweeping ketchup stain. With my head exploding, I stumbled through the door. The telephone receiver sat on an end table.

"Hello?" I sounded awful.

"Iss this Mister John?" a man asked in an accented, professional-sounding voice.

"Yes. Can I help you?"

"Mister Henry sayss you are now going to teach the men at the pharmacy English. Can you come tomorrow?"

"Uh, sure." I didn't even know what day of the week it was. "What part of town are you in?"

"What? Mister Henry tellss me he hass left you very clear information about where we are located," he sighed impatiently. Then he gave the address, which did me little good because I had no pen or paper. He responded curtly to other basics such as, "What time do we start?" and "How many people will I teach?" Nearly set to get off the phone, a final, important question occurred to me.

"What is your name?"

Dial tone followed an exasperated groan. I sat, stymied for the next move. Teaching? Tomorrow? At seven o'clock in the morning? This was a very bad development. Instinctively, I walked down the hall to purchase some beer, but found the liquor vendor's door locked. Juddering almost uncontrollably, I walked back to the kitchen. There was still a cup of coffee left in the urn. I gagged on the hours-old brew and Coffee-Mate when Raphael bounded into the room with a broad grin on his face and a fat joint in his hand. Would I care for a blast?

We inhaled smoke from the coarse Colombian weed as Raphael hit play on an album by Portishead. The musical backdrop laid down by hipsters in Bogotá departed far from the rock 'n roll that had blared when I came of age. I had never heard Portishead until a week before, but quickly grew to love the nervous-breakdown-style vocals and trance guitar soundtrack. All the gringos at the Platypus were partying to techno. In that atmosphere of trip-hop sounds, we sucked back the joint in short order. Overjoyed, I watched Raphael retrieve a plastic bag containing more pot. He deposited three brownish-green buds into a pipe and passed it to me.

"Here," he said, "I knew you could use this after last night."

Fear edged in. This was one of the worst parts about the backend of a bender: piecing together the story of the previous night. I sipped my coffee and tried to keep cool.

"I remember heading out somewhere. Did you come, too?"

"No. I was drinking beer with those Israeli guys when you came back at three in the morning. You were all drooly-faced – couldn't even talk! Some Irish fellows kept saying you found the cheapest booze in Bogotá. You had a half-done bottle of rum and one of the Israelis asked for a drink. But you just kept holding onto the bottle and staring at it. Man, you were super-hammered!"

I didn't like where this was going. Code among gringos was to share whatever intoxicants were available. That I didn't come across right away was bad news. Raphael continued.

"Those Irish guys tried to get it out of your hands, but you would not let go. You wrestled and the bottle smashed on the floor. Some of it splashed in the eye of the guy who asked for a drink and he was pretty mad. There was a plastic ketchup bottle on the table, so he opened it up and squirted it all over you. It was hilarious! I can see you haven't changed your shirt yet."

This was a brutal report.

"Uh, so, then what happened?"

"Not too much. The Irish guys were pissed about the rum, but everybody thought the ketchup squirt was funny. You kept staring at the smashed bottle before going to bed. I think it's okay, though. I talked to them this morning. Nobody is mad anymore."

The humiliation of having acted the drunken fool stung like it always did, but Raphael's pot eased the pain. Then I realized the time:

Nearly two in the afternoon and I'd been awake only half-an-hour. Turmoil hacked through the marijuana smokescreen. I had no idea how I was going to get it together to teach the next day. Stoned and in near-total despair, I thanked Raphael and returned to my room in hopes of finding Henry's papers.

Henry had been thorough in his preparations. A sheaf of papers detailed the instruction of the pharmacy class to-date, indicating a progressive grammar scheme. The thought of having to teach it threw me into a conniption. I could easily get across some general ideas, but explaining the technical side of the language would only sink into a labour of ignorance. I foresaw a good deal of faking it. Still, a glimmer of confidence remained. Henry's note said there were only three people in the class. The spoken part should go smoothly and, hopefully, teaching the smaller class would prepare me for the gig at the college. I shuddered thinking about that one.

I didn't get drunk that day. Palpitating with alcoholic hysteria, I took to my bike. Winding past the columned legislature at Bolívar Plaza, then cycling back to the main drag, Jiménez Avenue, I cranked toward the business district. The city throbbed as suits hustled to meetings, street people begged below the glistening skyscrapers while cabbies honked and shouted from their dented-up taxis. Despite Bogotá's choking air pollution, getting back on my bicycle felt good, and I circled downtown for an hour. I found the pharmacy and returned to the hotel, where I noticed that a rosy colour had replaced my pallor and the shakes had eased.

That short respite from melancholy evaporated when the alarm clock buzzed me awake at six o'clock the next morning. I debated turning it off and slipping back into dreamland to avoid the day. Somehow, I discovered enough resolve to get up and fool myself into believing I could teach. The dash through morning traffic made me wish I'd taken the sleep option. Nothing could have prepared me for the bedlam of Bogotá's rush hour.

Trucks and buses motored helter skelter, while cabs and scooters juked and whizzed through perilously small gaps. Every thirty seconds a vehicle came close to knocking me down. I thought my number was up when two transport trucks converged on me. There was no way to get ahead of either one, or any hope they would pass instead of hitting me. At the last possible second, one of the drivers pulled back into his original 'lane,' which opened up just enough space for me to squeeze past. Despite the frenetic pace, the commute was taking longer than the previous day's test ride – dodging cars proved no quick job. Worries about getting there on time crept into the picture. Four blocks ahead and five minutes before class was to start, the pharmacy pulled into focus. Locking up at the bike rack outside, it occurred to me that I should ride to work only on days I felt lucky.

Three guys in their 20s sat around a fake woodgrain table, looking too bushy-tailed for that early hour. A round of introductions got things moving and tipped me to their English skills. One could barely speak the language, another knew some, and the third was nearly fluent. They all brought homework Henry had assigned them: identical worksheets completed at varying skill levels. I checked their answers and tried to figure out what the hell I was going to do with these dudes. The hour dragged as I extracted bits of conversation from them. The one with the most English dominated the discussion until I brought the other two into it. It moved along socially, but stank as a lesson.

That afternoon, I embarked on a crash course in Henry's grammar lessons. I learned more about the mechanics of English, but that did nothing to improve my teaching ability. The students became listless in the days that followed. If I ever had their attention, I was losing it. More concerning was the fact I'd never met the man who was supposedly in charge of paying me. Henry had jotted the name 'Eduardo' next to a phone number. When I called him, he said he'd pay me at the end of the following week. I'd heard likelier stories.

Suspect qualifications aside, I still hoped to grab the college job

116

and phoned the Dean persistently. His secretary eventually returned my call and asked me to come to the university to meet with the Assistant Dean. I bought a six-dollar pair of leather shoes, put on my only pair of long pants and reported to her the next afternoon. The setting was more formal than expected, the Assistant Dean apparently qualifying for a decent furniture budget. The desk, resting on plush carpeting, was solid hardwood. Framed degrees hung behind her high-backed chair. The yellow, red and blue Colombian flag drooped on a flagpole in the corner and the office smelled pleasantly of pipe smoke. I was relaxed, even though a slight institutional feel ran through the building – I disliked institutions. The Assistant Dean spoke gently accented English and carried herself with a crisp, business-like demeanour.

"What iss your area of specialissation?"

I panicked. This was supposed to be a done deal, not a job interview. I thought fast – something I've always done badly. Then I heard myself spin a long string of lies.

"Well, I was studying to become a priest before I left Vancouver."

The Assistant Dean beamed.

"Oh!" she said.

"Yes, I studied remedial Latin and the Bible at Our Lady of Eternal Misery seminary."

Not being Catholic or even remotely religious, I didn't know if that made sense. The Assistant Dean frowned – a bad omen.

"I left to do some volunteer work with lepers in Upper Volta, but a guy can only do that sort of thing for so long, you know. Don't get me wrong, hey, I'm always thinking of new ways to give to the needy. I'm just on sort of a 'finding myself' quest for the time-being. I'm not sure about returning to the seminary. Right now, I'm hoping to put my skills to work for anyone who can use my help."

"I see. I believe the last English teacher we had wass a businessman. The dean sayss he wass good at teaching business talk. Many of our students want to learn English so they can do well in commerce.

Are there special skillss you can bring?"

"Yes."

"What are they?"

I had to stall.

"How many people will I be teaching?"

"The class sise iss about 35 students."

"How well can they speak English?"

"Most have had some English lessonss. You should have no trouble communicating with them in your native language. Some of them should be able to speak English as well as you at the end of the course. So can you tell me some more about your qualificationss?"

"Well, like I say, I didn't finish priest school but I think, I mean, I know I can do a good job here. I've taught English before."

"Where did you do that?"

"I have another teaching job here in town. I also taught English to the lepers in Upper Volta. And I spent six months in Burma as a part of a group of priests in training who taught English to poor people over there."

"Can you bring me a ressume?"

"I don't have one."

"You don't have a ressume?"

"Well, I do, just not here. It's in Vancouver."

"Could you write one?"

"I guess I could do that."

"Good. Bring it in as soon as you can."

I said I would and got up to leave. The Assistant Dean shook my hand, sizing me up with a doubtful look. The meeting had taken maybe ten minutes and now I was on the hook for a resume. That was depressing, but I looked forward to concocting a fictitious account of the past five years. If they took the bait, they deserved to have me teaching their class.

Back at the hotel with a beer in hand, I scrawled out an embellishment of the Upper Volta lie. As I wrote, it occurred to me that using a fake work record based on helping destitute and disfigured Africans was probably in bad taste. But that bothered me only momentarily; I had never been accused of having good taste. The first and final draft of the resume said I had been in Upper Volta for a year. The magnanimous works were endless, my charity and teaching skills having gained reknown throughout the land. The fabrication grew even more odious as it shifted to Burma. My crack team of novice priests had achieved divinely inspired acts there, preaching the word of the saviour and teaching the Queen's English. I rounded out the opus of bullshit with the names of 'priests' who would furnish me with glowing references.

I returned later that afternoon to slide the resume under the Assistant Dean's door and then biked back through the market, where greasy street stalls were belching out a horrendous stench. Those standbys of Bogotá's culinary culture deep-fried everything from sausages to entire pigs in vats of boiling oil. The most offensive odour blew in from a 'hamburger' kiosk. Bogotá burgers were a pasty, pink salmagundi of mystery bits, flattened and dropped into the bubbling grease. I had tried them once and regretted it.

Stomach turning, I hurried to clear the block, rounding a corner where a blind man stood every time I had been in the area. He wore sunglasses and sang songs for coins. The guy always smiled as he delivered his tunes. I rode past him and looked for places I had not yet been. Looping about, I stopped for a man and his llama, both standing near the city's bullfighting ring. Laugh lines furrowed the man's bronze skin around his mouth and eyes. He wore a thick, red poncho and an old, bowler hat. The fellow had arranged some wooden carvings and painted pottery on the sidewalk. He took me by the arm and pointed to each of his wares. I made to leave, but he wouldn't let go. Nodding toward his pack animal, and then indicating my bike he said, "¿cambio?" The llama tender doubled over laughing, almost failing to get the last syllable out of his mouth. Swapping a llama for a bicycle was apparently the silliest thing possible. I smiled and mounted the bike, shaking my head over what I would do with a llama. Perhaps I came close to getting the joke.

Speeding past a pair of military transports in a rundown neighbourhood, soldiers peered at me from the backs of the canvas-covered trucks. Citywide, the army assembled in strength. Identification checks took place most days. But inspections in Bogotá were less frequent than on the highway, and tended to be more of a nuisance than a problem. Even so, it was best to avoid them and I kicked the ride into high gear, working against the stiff October wind.

I returned to the hotel feeling refreshed. Further afternoons spent riding tempered a high-strung fixation on my budding career as a fraud. The additional time on the bike also slowed my drinking. Days later, one of the hotel staff handed me a message from the Assistant Dean. I gulped. The note said to call her back. The Assistant Dean picked up immediately.

"There are enough students to start the class on Monday. Can you teach that night?"

"Uh, yeah."

"Good. It starts at seven o'clock. Pleesse be there at six-thirty."

"Okay. I'll see you then."

"No. The Dean will be there. He wants to meet you."

"Oh."

Click.

Monday night. That gave me the weekend to avert utter disaster. I also needed to track down Eduardo, the shady moneyman from the pharmacy job. I still had not been paid. But it was Friday afternoon and I wanted to get teaching off my mind; I decided a few beers were in order. Just a few. Even if the night got a little boozy, there was still the whole weekend to get the slosh off my brain. Yes, three or four beers, that would be the perfect number. I swore a silent oath to stop at no more than five, so I could spend the weekend nailing down a program for the class.

A queue was forming outside the hotel owner's bootlegging counter, and a boisterous hum reverberated in the hall. The gringos were fixing to get their drink on at my favourite bar. Raphael chatted up some new arrivals and two Danish babes giggled in anticipation. Others laughed at somebody's loud fart and I caught the tail end of a raunchy joke. This was top news. Controlled drinking be damned – hadn't I done well to lie low on the beer for the past few days? A good party was revving up. Was I just going to sit in my room and read? No. I had earned the right to get wasted. One of the Danish women smiled at me as she cracked open her beer.

"Hey, are you coming with us tonight?"

"I think I might be able to arrange something. Everyone's going to the little pub in the attic, right?"

"I think so. The clubs are so expensive and there's too much coke. I just want to drink some beer."

"Yeah, shit, let's hit the booze."

"Cool. Me and Tina and a few more of us are going out for chicken and chips first. Want to come?"

I couldn't refuse. We chatted until I made it to the front of the line, where I laid out the cash for six bottles of beer. While socking away three of them in my room, I noticed an unfamiliar set of bags on my bed. A new roommate had claimed my bunk. I tossed the stuff on the floor, locked the door and joined the table where beers were going down fast. Chicken and chips had to wait because two Brits were out scoring weed. Pot sounded great, but for the moment, I was content to lounge in a suspended reality with fellow alcoholics.

A proficient chess player sat directly across from me, drinking a beer. The player, a nuclear scientist from France, had already dealt me four or five vigorous thrashings. Feeling the bravado of two quick beers, I challenged him to another game. He accepted with a patronizing grin and we set up the board at an empty table. I moved decisively, taking several of his pieces early. That shook him up. But he mounted a comeback, which cost me a bishop and both knights.

The physicist's eyes were more often on the boozy Irish woman at the next table than on the board. That resulted in the forfeit of his queen and second rook. He gasped in genuine horror at the loss of the rook. Two pawns and a knight were all that stood between my heavy artillery and his king. The Frenchman was crushed, having expected yet another easy victory. I felt the magic of a good beer buzz about to crank up five notches with the exhilaration of a startling win.

But at the exact same time I grabbed the second rook from the scientist, the doorbell rang. The Platypus had two iron-grated security doors and someone was having a deuce of a time getting past them. A drinker from the other table got up to assist whoever was trying to get in, and my opponent stared at the hopeless cause on his side of the chessboard. The Frenchman held both hands outstretched, shaking his head, when the visitor staggered through the door and into the room, transforming his gait into a drunken Moonwalk. He spun and · grabbed at invisible supports in the air. Finding none, the big lush collapsed into the chessboard, knocking all the pieces to the floor.

"Aw, holy fuck man! I had that in the bag! Do you know how many times this guy has beaten me? Shit! I was two moves from my first win."

Dead air swallowed up the room. All heads turned. A barely perceptible upturn played at the corners of my opponent's lips. Then somebody laughed, reanimating the place and two guys lifted the inebriate up by his armpits. He kicked furiously, collapsing to the floor and booting one of his supporters in the jaw. The man struggled to find his feet and fell over, bellowing. One of the Germans translated that the sot wanted to get to his room. He spluttered out a room number and four guys got up, taking care as they dragged him toward a familiar door.

"Hey man, looks like you've got a new roommate. Ha ha!"

"Oh, shut your hole. All I can say is he better not screw with my stuff. Dammit."

The soiree was all snickers as a smiling figure approached.

"What to do about the chess match? The whole thing is on the floor."

"We'll call it a stalemate, you lucky prick. Let's get to the bar."

Years later, it occurred to me that we could have reset the board to its pre-wipe out state. But the beer flowed that night and somebody came back with a sack of weed. The bender was well underway – far greater comfort than winning at chess. Our boorish crowd drank like frat boys and the bar keep chased us out at daybreak. One of the maids at the Platypus, beginning her morning shift, shook her head in disgust as she unlocked the gate for a dozen, plastered gringos. Everyone headed to bed, myself included.

Struggling drunkenly to unlock my bedroom door, the smell of smoke wafted from underneath it. A yank tore the door open from the other side and a psychopathic stare greeted me. I'd forgotten about the chessboard crasher. Drug cooking paraphernalia was scattered about the room. My roommate was free-basing cocaine. He threw me a paranoid look and mumbled something in German. I explained in a slurred tone that I didn't speak the language. He switched to English.

"Zere vas a fire!"

It was true. The plastic garbage can that sat next to the bureau had been melted to its base. Lighters, empty plastic bags, a bottle of ether, plus a blackened spoon littered the bureau top.

"You must haff started it. You could haff burnt ze whole buildink down! You are fuckink crazy!" he rasped.

Stunned, I resorted to the alibi of having been at the bar all night. But my new roommate would have none of it.

"Zis iss very dangerous. I could haff died because of you. I am goink to report you to ze manager in ze morning. You are an azzhole. Now I'm finished all my cocaine but I still haff some more druks. Do you vant to get high?"

The freak unzipped a pocket on his backpack and pulled out a plastic drinking straw filled with tiny white balls. I still don't know what sort of dope it was, but he said he wouldn't need a lighter to partake of it. That was good enough for me. I sprawled on my bed and passed out.

The party rolled for the whole weekend. By Monday morning, I was sure that I had alcohol poisoning. Too ill to lecture the pharmacy class, I gave instructions that the students discuss the weekend in English. Five minutes into the 'exercise' one of the guys had a question for me.

"Iss it possible that Henry could come back? We like hiss teaching much better. I think we learned more and we had more fun."

"You liked Henry better than me?"

"Yes, much better," he said, the other two nodding in agreement.

"What can I do to make things better?"

"You must teach better."

"I'll work on that. For now, you guys need to get back to your chat about the weekend."

"But we are finished."

"Keep practicing. There's going to be a test on this tomorrow."

"A test?"

"Yeah, a test. So it would be a good idea to get back at it," I said, straining to keep the ugliness out of my voice.

On the bus back to the hotel, I sank into a low depression. The pharmacy students had had enough of me, and who could blame them? They were this close to exposing me as a con artist – a richly deserved comeuppance. Worse, I was supposed to teach that night at the university. I spent the rest of that day devising something that might work as a lesson plan, but the despair was insurmountable. My sickening hangover clung tenaciously, and the suicidal thoughts that so often hounded me after a heavy booze-fest resurfaced, dragging me down into a spiritual cesspool. For a moment, I understood how failure and the astounding pain of alcoholism had crushed my dad.

I pulled it together enough to arrive at the campus earlier than the six-thirty appointment with the Dean. He was not in his office, but I guessed he wouldn't have much trouble picking me out in the classroom. Already there were six or seven students in desks, poring over reading material. All of them turned to stare as I walked in.

124

Nervously averting eye contact, I grabbed the closest spot – a small-ish desk-and-chair in a row of student seating. There was a podium at the front of the room. A real teacher would have stood there, shuffling lecture notes, giving off at least a faint air of authority.

Students continued to file into the room, looking at me. It was quarter-to-the-hour and still no sign of the Dean. I had gotten half-way out of my seat to check his office again when a distinguished-looking man walked into the classroom. This had to be the Dean. But the newcomer did not look in my direction. Instead, he strode up to the podium, opened a briefcase and placed some note pages onto it. Had I misread the signs in the hallway and found the wrong room? Probably. Stressed out and swearing under my breath, I got up and headed for the door, nearly bowling over a short man in a suit coming the other way.

"Excuse me," I said.

"Yes, excuse you. Are you a teacher?"

It sounded like a trick question.

"Yes. I'm here to teach English."

"I think that's where you are wrong. Come with me."

We marched the length of the hallway, stopping only once we were inside the Dean's office.

"I'm the Dean. I read your resume. It looked impressive, but I made some phone calls to check on you because you sounded too good. As far as we can tell, you did not attend any seminary school in Vancouver. None of the Catholic churches we called had ever heard of your references. And nobody on the administrative staff, including myself, believes you ever worked with lepers in Africa. You may have travelled to Asia but it is clear you are lying to us about what you did there. So, as you have seen, we have hired a good teacher for the class. Now get out of here and don't come back or we'll call the police."

I said nothing and left fast. The time to get out of Bogotá was closing in. I didn't know what my next move would be, but it needed to be soon. One thing was certain: Teaching was out. Back at the Platypus,

I made a phone call to the enigmatic Eduardo.

"…Yeah, yeah, something's come up. I have to leave Bogotá tomorrow. Sorry about the short notice, but I need to get paid up."

"You are running out on the class and you want me to pay you tomorrow? Are you crayssee? What am I going to do about the students? You need to give me notice for such a thing."

"Hey, c'mon, Henry left all of a sudden and he got paid."

"No he didn't. He left an address in Quito where I will send him hiss money."

Had Henry really believed the cheque was in the mail? Bullshit.

"Hey man, it's only 50 bucks you owe me. How hard is it to get that kind of cash together?"

"It's part of the pay system. I can't pay you until payday."

"But I was supposed to get my money on Friday."

"That's not my fault. The man who runss the pay system wass sick last week and he'ss still not back to work yet."

That smelled as much like bullshit as my resume did. Payday was a mirage, so I decided to have some fun with Eduardo. Two prank phone callers from New York were making a name for themselves at that time, releasing CDs under the name of the 'Jerky Boys.' I improvised a timely rendering of their revue.

"Yeah, well it's probably good for your students I'm leaving. Have they mentioned anything about the beatings?"

"What beatingss?"

"Well, when they get an answer wrong – and believe me those morons get just about everything wrong – I rap 'em about the chin, chest and buttocks with a piece of copper tubing. They didn't say anything about that, eh?"

"Not yet!"

"Yeah, they started to get more answers right after they saw I wasn't fooling around. I've got a great technique for fixing the way they talk, too. If they screw up a word, I jam a piece of putty in their mouths and make 'em chew on it for a while. Then I tell 'em to take it out and repeat the sentence – they usually get it right after that. So you don't feel like paying me, eh? Maybe I should come over there and straighten you out!"

"You force them to chew poo-ty?"

"No, anal-zest, putty! Clean the shit out of your ears!"

"You are a terrible man!"

"Hey fart-lips, you're the one who doesn't pay! You're lucky I don't come over there with an air compressor hose and run it up your ass full blast!"

Eduardo hung up and I heaved a deep belly laugh, my septic moroseness having crept into remission. Even though teaching had netted me zero, I was relieved that I didn't have to do it anymore. This called for a beer. Part way into the bottle, it hit me that I could have told Eduardo he had a choice: Get my money together or I'd tell everyone at the Platypus not to deal with him. The threat of disrepute among potential employees might have changed his mind about paying me. Having performed the Jerky Boys' spiel now didn't seem quite so funny. My spirits revived when Raphael joined me for a drink. He planned to head for a Colombian island on the Caribbean in a couple of days. Others would tag along. The Danish women and the Irish clique were taking off, too.

I packed up and cashed one of my few remaining traveller's cheques the next day. From the bank, I walked over to Bolívar Plaza, admiring the facade and bell towers of the nearly 200-year-old Primada Cathedral. Schoolchildren laughed and chased each other and old men read newspapers on benches across from the Sagrario Chapel. Blocks away, I stopped outside a storefront with the Spanish word 'esperma' painted on the window. My depleted finances pushed me in the door. The business had a generic office look, though I'm not sure what I expected from a sperm bank, other than a more clinical air. Employees bustled about the place and it took ten minutes to flag someone down. I asked if anyone there spoke English. One person did, but I would have to wait.

That gave me time to think. The throngs of street kids in the city made me wonder why there was a demand for sperm donors at all. I figured it must be a middle-to-upper class thing. Maybe there were burgeoning numbers of young women who wanted children but no husband. Perhaps they wanted to choose the stock they would mix with their own, rather than adopting a street urchin. Whatever the reason, with so many poverty-stricken children around, I astonished myself that I had the moral turpitude to get paid for helping make another baby. Faking it at teaching was one thing; this was a new low. I mulled over the prospective life of such a child versus that of an unlucky kid in the slums. It didn't seem fair, especially when I remembered the hotel staff talking about how common glue sniffing was among street kids – youngsters fleeing broken homes or guerrilla conflict reduced to stealing to survive. Many bore scars said to have come from clashes with police. Cheap and plentiful glue dulled the pain. I had seen them myself, sad little ones with twitchy red eyes as young as eight or nine, wired on inhalants.

But I couldn't make a would-be mother accept one of those children. If she wanted my DNA, it was for sale. That raised the question of payment. How much per sample? No matter the going rate, it had to be more lucrative than teaching for free. A man interrupted my thoughts of a semen-based cash flow.

"Can I help you?"

"Yes, I'm here about the sperm samples."

"Are you a farmer?"

"No. Are you looking for farmers to, ah, um, make samples?"

"Sir?"

They must have wanted farmers' sperm because of their healthy, outdoor lifestyles. I assured the man I was in top shape.

"I exercise every day – I ride a bicycle all over the place. I'm completely healthy."

"That's good for you, sir."

"Right. So, um, about the samples, how much do you pay?"

The man gave me the most peculiar look.

"If I can ask, sir, if you're not a farmer, whose sperm will you sell?"

This was getting weird. His English was near perfect, but something had to have been getting lost in translation.

"I'm not sure what the laws are in this country, but it seems strange to me that it would be legal to sell another man's sperm. I don't know why it's so important that you get farmers to supply it. I'm sure that my own sperm is as good as any you're gonna find. So can we get started here?"

"Just a minute, sir."

Semen collection and storage must have required a team of professionals. Why else would all the employees have come into the foyer? The office worker began to speak in Spanish once they had assembled. I understood pieces of his translation, but not enough to figure out why people were chuckling. As the retelling reached a crescendo, everyone but me howled with laughter. The merriment had not yet died down when the interpreter spoke again.

"Sir, we are a small company that trades in semen – bull semen! Would you care to buy some?"

They guffawed me into the street. Very funny indeed. As I made myself scarce, a mime was busying himself on the sidewalk. He exaggerated the gaits of passers-by, aping their characteristics. I watched as he stealthily made his way behind a businessman, a grandmother and an off-duty bus driver, turning farcical caricatures. Crowds laughed and then dispersed as the grease-painted harlequin sought out his next victim. His targets discovered they'd been had when people bunched together to goggle and snigger at them. But the clown was quick. Just as a group stopped to observe his pantomimes, the target would pivot, trying to catch him in the act. By then the mime had found someone else to bother. The speedy turnaround made the whole act even funnier.

Twenty minutes were enough of the Marcel Marceau impersonator's antics. I headed back toward the hotel, stopping first at a street stall that sold trinkets. A grey-haired woman smiled toothlessly as I inspected the necklaces, lockets and Spanish-language bibles. Deciding against a purchase, I moved on. Within seconds, the mime got the drop on me. People stared, grinning in my direction. I played dumb and continued my naturally loping, slouched stride as a crowd of 30 giggled. I spun on my heels.

"Gotcha!" I shouted. My move was quicker than the clown's, startling him. The hilarity struck a fever pitch – I got a better laugh than the mime! The joker stood, shocked, apparently, out of ammunition. His eyes burned with anger. The mime did not like the turnabout, but he cut his losses and fumed down the avenue.

Not content to take the win and split, I went after a wider margin of victory. The mime moved fast to vanish from where he'd been vanquished, but I followed him. Little did I know I had merely won the battle, irreversibly turning a corner leading to tragic defeat. With speed, I manoeuvred through the crowd to a spot right behind the clown, mimicking his fleet-footed movements. The veteran performer knew I had tailed him when a tittering cluster of people blew my cover. The enraged mime spiralled to face me. He stopped, searching for an idea. Then he reached out to shake my hand and pointed across the street. I was still looking when the jester slipped behind me, grabbed my shorts and pulled them down to the sidewalk.

The entire street erupted in uproarious howls. In mere minutes, the most embarrassing moment of my life had been topped. But it wasn't quite over. As the mime basked in his coup de grace, I noticed that my underwear remained in position. Making no move to retrieve my shorts, I turned my backside toward the little imp, yanked down my undergarment and revealed my ass to him and everyone else on the block. The crowd's laughter turned to gasps. Smiles evaporated and the gathering broke up. Colombians sure have a fickle sense of humour. I replaced the dropped laundry, scanned the area for military police and boogied back to the Platypus.

The usual liquor fiends were drinking beer in the parlour, marking a special occasion: It was Halloween and the kegs were open. Those who'd planned to leave put off departure for one final bender. The Last Drunk led to our dark little bar following a gallon of primers. Tiny trick-or-treaters in ghost, goblin and faerie attire zigzagged the streets. Murders of made-up and bolted Frankensteins shuffled to evening festivities. Even at the bar, costumed creeps threw back cheap beer. A stranger made his way up to our haunt, sporting demonic horns, a red cape and a pitchfork. Satan pointed downward – to Hell! Then he let out a big laugh and ordered a beer. His accent positively made him Irish. The 50-year-old devil sat down to join the rest of the jolly drunks.

The demon enjoyed himself, as tunes by Black Sabbath drifted from a set of unseen speakers. It turned out the ghoul had information about a move I had thought about making – to a sex farm. The Platypus Hotel kept a guest book where people could log their Colombian adventures. The sex farm was a theme throughout.

A group of Irish ex-pats ran the place, about a day's bus ride out of Bogotá. Logbook entries told of a work-for-food commune in the mountains, where hippie-style free love values reigned. So far on the road, there had been no getting it on. The only thing even remotely close to it was a strikeout out with one of the Danish cuties at the Platypus. Even the sperm bank had turned into a bust.

I asked the Irish Beelzebub if he'd heard of some of his country-folk having a swinging good time in the jungle. He had – sort of.

"Look man, I know that crew. They're a bit off the wall, but mostly harmless. No end of shite gets spread around this fuckin' city about 'em, though. It's been awhile since I've been to the commune. They work hard and scream a bunch. I've heard there's a bunch of fuckin' goin' on up there, but I can't say whether there's any truth in that. Personally, I doubt it."

"What do you mean they 'scream'?"

"That's their philosophy. They scream. Some call 'em the Scream-ers. It's supposed to be therapeutic. I saw it once, but I still don't know what the point of it is. Seems fucked up to me."

"Are you sure there are no commune babes looking to get laid? I've read that things are pretty loose down there."

"You fuckin' read that? Don't tell me there's a bloody book about this shite now! Fucksakes!"

I explained about the logbook.

"Fuckin' hell. Some people'll write anything to get a kick. I can say that if you go, don't be expectin' any beauties to come for ya. Last time I was there, I saw one uglier than a pig's arse! And if there are any sweeties, I'd bet they're more discreet than these fuckin' logbook scribbles yer talking about. These sorts of stories have been circulating for years. Look man, these people are farmers and they bust their arses gettin' crops in. They're out in the jungle to avoid society. They make their own rules. Maybe the women are givin' it away, maybe not."

I shot back a glass of rotgut and considered what the devil had to say.

"When were you at the farm last?"

"Maybe eight years ago. We got right merry on their homemade wine. If they're still makin' that stuff, yer in fer a good pisser."

Things can change on a sex farm over eight years, but it didn't matter at the moment – we ripped it up until sunrise. Everyone was weary from too much drinking. One of the Irishmen even complained of gout as we stumbled back. When I woke up the next afternoon, I couldn't stand it any more. Slurping back a coffee with red-eyed, morning-after regret, I longed for the intoxicated exuberance of the previous night. The clock read 3:30 PM and I was determined to get out of town that day. I finished my cup and clicked the panniers onto my bike with a new purpose. Conflicting reports be damned, I decided at that moment to head to the sex farm.

I'm a loser baby, so why don't you kill me? – BECK

The endless cruise through the southern night had hypnotized me into driving by rote, which touched off an uproar: James, if he ever had actually been asleep, was not any longer.

"Jesus Christ! Stay out of the left-hand lane! It's for passing only. I know you're trying to make time, but that's not what the lane is for. WATCH OUT! Fuck man, signal when you're switching lanes. Holy crap. This is ridiculous. Pull over at the next exit. I'll drive."

James fiddled with the tuning knob on the radio, replacing the hockey game with country and western music. I couldn't tell whether my driving truly irritated him or if he was merely coming unravelled. Either way, I liked it better when he pretended to be asleep. An exit off Highway 49 led toward a town called Florence – still miles from the Mississippi capital of Jackson. I would happily turn the wheel over to James before connecting with Interstate 20, which would take us all the way to Dallas. Too tired to comment on his tirade, I thought about getting to Amarillo, not wanting a battle of wills to end my ride. The ride-whore mentality had become a part of me.

I pulled into a gas station just outside of Florence and handed the keys to James, who scowled as he took the driver's seat. He flicked the turn signal with an angry snap and we faded back into the nighttime highway traffic. A streetlight provided a glimpse of James' profile; his irate expression made him look like Yosemite Sam. He drove in dour quiet for three hours before stopping to use the bathroom. I took one more stint at the wheel after that, James cursing and tossing up his hands in a livid hand-jive the whole time.

Dawn broke as we hit the Dallas city limits with James making good time. He had already chosen the route to his brother's house. That meant my half-dozing brain did not have to assist in deciphering the tangle of off-ramps leading to the city. James said the directions were straightforward, and I hoped that meant his amiable side would take over.

"Let's see, I know we want to take a certain exit to get off I-20. I remember clearly which one it is – I can count down the exit numbers from here."

That sounded like a great idea.

"Waitaminit! What's this? When did they change the numbers? Now I don't know where to make the turnoff. Shit! I'm gonna have to guess. Dammit!"

I sat on edge. James grimaced and selected a random exit.

"I really hope this is the right one or I'm gonna blow my top. I'm such an idiot for not checking. Shit. Let's see now, this area looks familiar. Doesn't Edward just live a few blocks from here?"

His tone rose and fell between optimistic peaks and seething valleys. I could understand it – driving around with only a general idea of where you're going is frustrating. But losing your way entirely is much worse.

"Bugger! I five-star screwed us. The only reason I recognize this place is because Edward and I came to this neighbourhood to eat a couple of times. Goddammit! We're gonna be late picking him up and I still don't know which exit we need. I'm such an idiot!"

James pulled over and asked for directions.

"The guy at the gas station says we have to loop back around and keep going for nine more exits until we see a McDonald's on the right – I'll know where I'm going from there. But it's still at least 20 minutes away and we're gonna be really late. I'm so pissed off I could punch a hole through the fucking windshield! I need to get out of this shit mood by the time we pick up Edward, so I'm going to swear at myself. Don't interrupt or try to stop me."

James embarked on a unique barrage of crazy. He bellowed that he was a "shit-stained asshole," an "aborted piss-fart" and a "moron who should be sent to idiot purgatory for a 1,000 years." He half-screamed, half-choked out run-on sentences such as, 'Shovel me down a bowl of piss on potted meat without any goddamned saltines on a flyboy fuck march past the fucking mess hall shit on my balls after a shower and every other kind of fart-flavoured piss shit in the cockpit fuck my helmet with sequined semen and fuck fuck fuuuuuck!' James raved without a break for ten minutes, coining new swear words the whole time. It was a disturbing, yet magnificent, performance. When I thought he was finished, I told him he shouldn't be so hard on himself.

"Hey, I told you not stop me. I'm a complete fuck-shit for screwing this up! Don't mess with me – not right now."

It was tough to argue with him. He seemed to enjoy it. The only difficulty was that I had to stifle snorts of laughter when he came up with awe-inspiring paragraphs of original profanity. I did not want James to catch me laughing at him. Minutes later, we arrived at his brother's door. James rounded out the festival of curses by denouncing himself as a fiddly-fuck retard. Then he put a smile on his face and jumped out of his truck. His brother was waiting in the doorway.

"Hey Edward! You're looking great!"

James approached his brother with a hurried step.

"Hey brother – great to see you!"

The two men embraced warmly as I stood on the sidewalk. Edward was ten years older than James. The more mature brother moved with an easy manner. Right away, the tension relaxed its way out of James' face. James apologized for being late but Edward said he hadn't noticed the time.

As heart-warming as the reunion was, it represented an incontestable downside for me: I would soon be riding in the back of the truck. I remembered the woebegone straggler James picked up in Florida. At the time, I thought it better him than me riding in that deep freeze. Now it was my turn to make the best of a six-hour drive across the frosty plains. James had mentioned that he would let me bundle up in his military-issue sleeping bag as we made the nearly 400 miles to Northwest Texas, but this did little to lift my spirits.

"Hey, come over and meet my brother!"

James had socked away the foul energy that dominated the last half-hour of our driving time. Just moments next to his brother made him look looser, happier. James introduced us and explained how we came to be travelling together. I shook hands with Edward, a potbellied, jovial-sounding man.

"So James picked you up hitchhiking, huh? That sure sounds like my brother, heh, heh. Good to have you along with us to Amarillo. It's bound to get cold back there. I'll make sure my little brother gets us there as quick as a roadrunner!" he said with a wink.

James produced an army green sleeping bag.

"Here you go. Zip up and lie flat. We don't want any Texas Rangers to see you back there."

I took off my shoes and snuggled into the cover. It was a whole lot cosier than the thin rag I still had rolled up in my panniers. The sleeping bag shielded me against the wind until James veered his truck out of the city and onto the open road. Things got really cold once we geared up to cruising speed. The wind cut right through the nylon and bird-down filling, icy blasts whipping my face. I dreaded the idea of an entire day of this. I couldn't even sit up to take in the sights for fear of getting busted – no telling what sort of trouble the Texas authorities would cook up for me if they pulled us over. I rode in the cold while trying to beat back the terror of what lay in store when the ride ended. I also had a heavy jones going on for some liquor. It had been at least four days since I'd had a drink.

136

Alcohol addiction revved into overdrive: the all-encompassing thirst; the ache to go berserk in some godforsaken bar; the illusion I could escape into a bright future with a rousing drunk. Therein lay a grave conflict. I had thought this now off-the-rails odyssey would deepen my sympathy for others. Part of the idea had been to gain out-of-hemisphere perspective while shedding the focus on personal minutiae. Instead, I shocked myself with the depraved sorrow I felt for my current state. Damn, I could have used some liquor – its warm, liquid hand being the only thing that faithfully detoured me from the lowest thoughts.

Suicide, always lurking somewhere in the back of my mind, showed its mocking face that day. Reasons to go on were sparse – having put everything I had financially, mentally and physically into hard travelling, but grandly failing to accomplish anything. I indulged in self-pity, never for a moment doubting how pathetic it was. I thought of my family, and how if I ever got back home I would return to them broke, scraggly and changed only for the worse. What would I do for work? Surely I was too much of a reprobate to give college a shot – a future of living in cheap apartments, an infinite string of shitty jobs, asshole bosses, rounded out with unending Cheez-Whiz-sandwich and frozen fish-stick dinners loomed as inevitable. I didn't want to hang around for that. But I hit a suicide paradox: Afraid to go on living, I was also too scared to jump out of the back of a moving truck or do whatever the hell it is people do to kill themselves – too cowardly to live, too cowardly to die. That meant there was nothing to do. I gritted my teeth, shivered and hoped.

Soon enough, another troublesome thought occurred to me. We crossed the Mississippi River the night before and I hadn't even noticed. I must have been asleep when we drove over the bridge into Louisiana. Even if I had been awake, I wouldn't have asked James to stop. But I was gutted that I'd passed over the great river without being aware of it. I thought back to the months in South America. At least then I knew where I was most of the time. I remembered making a crucial decision after some weeks in Ecuador; I could use the remainder of my cash to buy a plane ticket home, or I could sail the Amazon River. I set out for the massive artery in the heart of the continent because I absolutely had to see Nature's bloodline. And when I got to the Amazon, there was no doubt about the location – never a chance of missing it.

When your flood surrounds me and the waters burst and come, who knows the things that I have felt, who knows what I have done?
– NOMEANSNO

My bicycle was all but wrecked. The old frame, cheap parts and my monumental lack of mechanical acumen conspired to ensure the last time I rode it was through the streets of Chiclayo in Northern Peru. I didn't know that at the time, so I kept the moribund thing with me for another 800 miles. It rolled well enough to tote my gear and I still had it when I crossed the border into Brazil. But I think I knew the old mount had given up the ghost when I bussed it to the Peruvian port town of Yurimaguas, where the road ended and the river began.

Yurimaguas sat on an Amazon tributary known as the Huallaga. With the jungle hemming the place to the river, parts of it were cosy. But ugly gaps scarred the tree line, stands of ceiba trees cut away to make room on the muddy banks for ship service and repair. At the same time, the jungle threatened to reclaim the town: Swaths of cinchona trees and undergrowth encroached upon the neighbourhoods of tin-roofed houses. Chainsaws buzzed continually to keep Yurimaguas' backyards from succumbing to the thickets. The place sweltered in tropical steam, with the humidity soaking my shirt before I made it halfway from my hotel to the docks. Mini-cabs darted toward the waterfront, and a man pedalled a bike with his mother doubling side-saddle.

Dockside, heavy, engine oil made rainbows on the river. The swirling patches of grime lapped against the pier as I set my compass home. I needed to sail to Manaus, about two-thirds of the way down the Amazon. I'd grab a bus from there, north through Brazil to Venezuela, and hope the rumours were true about 100 dollar flights from Caracas to Miami. I put my search for a boat on hold when I blundered into a bar. Empty beer bottles crowded a table where four men were beginning to get drunk. I ordered a beer and sat down, alone.

I'd taken only a swig when the foursome asked me to belly up to their table. They were a slow-moving crew and I'm not sure what they did other than drink beer. But they had the low-down on the docks, and told me about vessels heading downriver. I groaned at the news one had departed for Iquitos two hours earlier, and that nothing else was leaving for two more days. Anxiety hit: Finances were slender and the time for lazing in sunny nowhere was past. I peeled the label off my bottle and stared at the Huallaga.

Worry receded with the second round, and a drinking game I had interrupted resumed. One of the four would pour a dribble of beer into a glass and slam it back like whiskey before passing the bottle. I had to hold back a self-assured smirk when they asked me to join in. It was a waste of beer and an amateur way to get hammered. But I played anyway. I looked around the table listening to the rolling Spanish the party spoke as they got louder and drunker. None of them sported the look of the grizzled river rats I'd seen flitting about the boatyards. They were pasty, despite the beating sun, and there were no tell-tale signs any of them knew about hard work.

Within an hour, the medium-sized collection of empty bottles on the table became a large one. There had been no clear accounting each time beer was served, but a sinking feeling began to gnaw that a plan was in the works for me to pick up the tab. I gathered my wits and was about to move on when the young woman who had been serving the beer sat down behind me and started to play with my hair.

The girl, about 18 with a beautiful smile, ignored the greasy state of my mop and began turning it into braids. She giggled as she stroked the back of my neck, and I was happy to let her continue. The lovely barmaid paused only for a quick trip to the refrigerator to grab a cerveza that I didn't ask for. She collected money from me, opened the beer and poured it into the glass used for the drinking game. One of the guys guzzled it, refilled the cup and passed it to his friend.

I knew they were hustling me, but it wasn't until later that I figured out the other drinkers were signalling the waitress as she fiddled with my hair. I'd almost forgotten what the touch of a woman felt like, and being played for a sucker felt pretty good at the time. I might have run a tab all afternoon, but the veteran drunk in me knew better than to let this go any further. I reached behind my neck and squeezed the woman's hand, holding it for longer than was necessary to tell her it was time to stop.

The half-drunk idlers yelled for me to stay when I tried to settle up. Seeing that I insisted on getting out, they argued with me over the bottom-line. The barmaid put on her best pout and handed me a bill for nine beers. I had drunk no more than five, and spirited haggling reduced the tally to seven. The enterprising server pocketed the money and swung her hips back into the tumbledown shack where she kept the cervezas. I wondered if her duties ended with slinging beer. A creepy sexual energy had crossed between the four layabouts and the young woman. I hoped she was not forced to do any dirty work other than bamboozling rubes.

A longshoreman confirmed what the bar crowd had said – indeed, a ferry was supposed to head downriver in two days. Nobody in town sold tickets, however. Passengers paid once they boarded. The only trouble with that was that the boat sailed at mysterious hours. If you wanted to travel, you showed up quayside and waited.

There was little to do in Yurimaguas other than sweat and mark time. I took to sitting on a wharf, watching a fisherman. He stood on a bank across the river, heaving his net with two-handed throws. He had no luck for the first three or four casts, but eventually hauled in a small school of flapping fish. The man picked them out and flung the net back into the river. I guessed that he chose the opposite shore because of all the noise on the town side. The whine of power tools used in boat repair and the churn of motors on the skiffs and tugs easing in to port probably chased away the fish.

A whistle finally sounded on my third day in Yurimaguas. Dozens of people rushed all at once to form a jostling queue for the rickety boat limping toward shore. Young men pushed each other to get to the front of the line, tripping one guy face first onto the wharf. Elderly couples looked for a way into the line-up without getting bumped as two shore workers yelled for everyone to clear the way. A hubbub of squealing barnyard animals, darting children and scolding mothers worked its way up the gangplank as soon as the vessel moored.

Dodging voyagers going ashore, I bulled my bike through knots of passengers scrambling for position on deck. Most of the chaos died down after everything had been stowed on board. By then, the boat, an aged, 100-foot long rusting shell had become a sea of colourful hammocks. I strung my own red bolt of canvas between two metal posts. Space was at a premium. Moving from one's hammock to, say, the bathroom involved wedging through square inches brimming with neighbours. The smell of pigs and goats from below decks permeated the air, and the terrified animals shrieked unceasingly. Deckhands slipped the ropes from the greased pilings and the whistle blew. An older man made the sign of the cross as the boat began to chug downriver.

Thriving jungle arrests the eye when travelling in that part of the world. The canopy of ceiba trees, vines, flowers and undergrowth blurs into an Impressionist painting of green after a spell of gazing. Two days on murky and dark tributaries led to the Amazon River. Our captain guided us into the docks at Iquitos late in the afternoon. Residents said it was the largest city in the world with no road links.

I had never imagined such a place. People from all over the

Amazon jammed the city's bazaars. The shantytown market in the Belén neighbourhood stood out as positively strange. Huts floated on river rafts or sat, mired in mud, ready to ride the next high tide. Kiosks stood beside sludgy pathways, offering up jungle flora and fauna. Vendors shouted, and shop merchants chatted over barbequed monkey and piranha dinner specials. The seared flesh actually smelled like it would be tasty with a squirt of chipotle sauce. Turtles and still-flopping catfish were on the block, and a row of stalls displayed herbs and medicinal plants picked in the jungle. At the other end of the market, dozens of baby caimans were up for grabs. The refreshing variety was limitless; a guy even tried to sell me a baby sloth for 10 bucks.

Iquitos and its Belén district had lots in common with other South American cities: vivacious residents; exhaust-spewing mini-cabs; and, the smell of garbage in the streets. But the striking differences continued. Landlocked Quito and Bogotá had massive slum areas, parts of which I visited. The Belén slum was right in the river. A fluid, transient sense linked to its propinquity to the Amazon gave the settlement a feel of even greater destitution than those other shantytowns. The timeless, flowing giant cast all else around it in a light of impermanence, and it could wash away everything except poverty.

The trappings of the jungle added another layer to Belén's look. Huts roofed with thatching gathered in the woods were common there. The use of vegetation to complete a home signalled both ingenuity and poverty. A thousand of these broken-down shacks created a low-rise, haystack skyline. Some of the dwellings rested on stilts over reeking, open sewers running in ditches 10 feet across. Dirty, naked children played next to the foul water. I hurried through that end of the neighbourhood and didn't look back.

The slow drift of the river also carried base desire along with it, washing up human flotsam and jetsam onto the docks. Brothels were popular. A sandwich board outside one 'hotel' featured a cartoon rendering of a smiling, naked woman. Common decency suggested looking elsewhere for a bed, but I needed someplace cheap. I checked into a depressing little room, where the only separation from the next one was a thin piece of plywood that stopped three feet short of the ceiling. A rubber sheet covered the bed, which canted noticeably downward – perhaps an effective means to prevent any hourly renter from basking overlong in his afterglow.

Two dismal nights passed with lots of indiscreet traffic moving through. On the morning the ship to the Brazilian line was ready to sail, I made sure to leave the rotten cathouse/hotel at first light to get dockside. The Enith was slightly bigger and a good number of years older than the boat that made the Iquitos run. I had grave doubts it could navigate such a huge chunk of the Amazon. The rusted hulk was stuffed even fuller than the last ferry, its hull dipping deep into the river.

Starting slowly and never gaining any momentum, the boat put-putted its way through a jerky whistle stop schedule. I grumbled at the dawdling pace, dreading three days of it. The captain meandered the ancient ship into village after village. Supremely bored as the ferry docked yet again, I climbed three decks up. My aim was to plummet into the Amazon. Gripped by vertigo, an audience assembled as I hesitated. Some shouted encouragement and others waved their arms and shook their heads trying to get me to climb off the roof.

The view from the top was brilliant. The sky blazed blue, clashing with the jungle's deep green. The Amazon, now beginning to widen considerably, was the familiar muddy brown I had stared at for hundreds of miles. I trembled at the idea of barrelling into the hugest river in the world, and considered reasons for abandoning the plan. The most compelling was the possibility of being eaten by piranhas. I had seen the fish in aquariums, and their fangs looked dangerous. Electric eels are also supposed to live in the Amazon, along with caimans and who knew how many other deadly river-going beasts. This must have been what the "don't jump" crowd was fussing about.

I pushed those creatures out of my mind, drew a deep breath and jumped. A second later, I splashed into the Amazon, its warm current welling about my body. Sinking fear instantly set in. Were piranhas moving up from the depths to attack me? People on deck shouted as I tried to look unconcerned swimming back.

Sailors had moored The Enith to another boat, linking the two with a gangplank. Claustrophobia swarmed as I knifed through the oil-slicked water in the four-foot space between the ships. I grabbed one of the buoys dangling from the Enith and heaved on the rope, half-expecting someone on board to offer a hand. No one did and the effort nearly made me pass out. Back on the boat, my legs buckled but I steadied myself. Were these the lingering effects of my earlier bout with dysentery? I wasn't sure – my field of vision blurred and I nearly threw up when a man approached me. He spoke in clear English.

"That was a good jump from the top of the boat. Are you all right?"

"I'm okay."

"Do you know what people here fear most from the river?"

"Piranhas?"

"No. Piranhas are bad fish and they must be avoided. But there is something much more dangerous in this water. "Do you know of the candirú fish?"

I did not.

"They are a tiny parasite that can swim into your penis. It is very dangerous to relieve yourself while in the river. That is how the candirú enters your body. Once inside it opens spiky bones to dig into your penis. The only way to remove it is to cut off your manhood."

A shudder wriggled through my body. A penis destroying fish? Could this be true? It didn't feel like I had a spiked fish in my penis. I attempted an offhand reach toward my bits.

"Don't worry," said the man, "you would certainly know by now if the candirú was in your penis. I would caution against another swim in this river."

Wet and feeling sick, I weaved back to my hammock. There was now even less room to move, as a woman and her three small children had boarded at this stop and set up next to me. The woman had skilfully threaded two hammocks through the webs of canvas and cords strung from every post. But the sounds from three feet away told me that my place had gone bad. Deep, hacking coughs tore from the new rider's chest, while her children zipped under and around the maze of hammocks. The woman sprawled listlessly with her limbs flopped over the sides of the makeshift bed. I believe she had tuberculosis.

Lying motionless, she covered her head with a towel. Setting up the space for her children must have cost her great effort. I felt sorry for her, but I was more worried for myself – the last thing I needed was TB Another ghastly burst of coughing warned of disease all around the woman's hammock. The beige towel covering her face soon drenched through. At first I thought she was sweating into the towel. A closer look revealed splotches of blood. This woman had to be dying. Yet her kids laughed, in high spirits about the boat ride.

Unable to stand the horrible coughing sounds, and still rocked by thoughts of the candirú, I moped around the decks in a squeamish funk. The ship had resumed its sluggish chug downriver. Through the tangle of hammocks, I could see the kids playing together. A man next to them pitched a candy wrapper overboard. Then the little ones gathered some debris to hurl into the water, but I walked over to intervene. The oldest one got his bit of garbage over the side before I could do anything about it. With a smile, I snagged the newspaper the middle child was about to lob, turning it into an impromptu dunce cap. All three laughed.

The kids then roped me into a rowdy game of tag that quickly slid into a fracas with other riders. Halting the sport before someone ratted us out to the captain, I moved over to the starboard side to look at something toward shore. There was movement in the water where a dark tributary emptied into the Amazon. I gasped. Eight or ten pink dolphins were swimming where the rivers met! The sick woman's children ran up behind me, giggling in delight when they saw what I saw.

The dolphins leaped through the air and back into the water. Their bottlenoses and pink flippers were a surreal joy to behold. Other passengers pointed and chattered. Inside of a minute, nearly everyone aboard leaned over the rail to watch them splash and flip. A terrific energy worked through the starboard side as the ship bobbed alongside the dolphins. The children knew it was magical, and their laughter blended in with the hushed tones of the adults. We could do nothing but watch in amazement.

The boat, slow as it was, worked its way past the beautiful creatures too quickly. Years later, I reflected that the dream I chased through South America crested at the sight of the dolphins. At the time, drifting ahead of them, I was torn between wanting to keep watching and needing to use the bathroom. I had been putting off that dreadful moment. The facilities on the last boat were repulsive. The flies and retch-inducing stench made me doubt whether any deck-swabber had ever done duty there. With that in mind, I had limited myself to three hurried uses.

The bathroom door on the Enith banged open and shut as the ship eased along the river. Rank odours drifted outward each time the door popped open. I held my breath and stepped inside. The commode was small, rusted and alive with flies. A pile of human waste almost topped the rim. This did nothing to ease my still unsettled stomach. I prepared for as quick a turnaround as possible. Breathing through my mouth, things moved speedily and according to plan. But the completion of the exercise went horribly wrong. Something moved. Something not quite inside me – at least not any more – was struggling to get out by its own power. The silent scream that wells up in nightmares made a desperate grab for traction but produced no sound. The only thing coming out of me was from the other end.

It felt like my insides had turned to liquid and my muscles no longer controlled anything. Squirming came from my rear and terror blasted through every capillary. Barely able to keep my legs from collapsing, I grabbed behind myself and pulled. Fourteen inches of white, writhing parasite as thick as a nickel slithered out of my hands into the abyss of the toilet. Frantic paralysis riveted me in place.

A rattling knock at the door shocked me into action. In utter horror, I cleaned myself up quickly and bolted past the person waiting. Dear God! What was that thing? How many more of them were there? How was I going to get the cure? Drowning in adrenaline, I plunged into my hammock, wanting to rip off my skin.

A fix would have to wait. The sailing still had two overnight segments to go before docking at the Brazilian border on Christmas Eve. I wondered if there were any doctors in that little crossover town, or if they'd even be open. Failing that, it was at least another four days to Manaus. More nausea struck when a weird sight paraded past. I had not heard the dinner bell, but people were heading to the outer decks with oddly dressed plates. Supper was piranha. The saucer-eyed fish with the gruesome fangs stared as diners cut into them. There was plantain on the side and warm Coke to drink.

I couldn't think about eating. My squirming passengers must have latched on through the local food in the first place. I thought back. I had made the stupid decision to drink a mouthful of tap water in Mexico in the hope of becoming acclimatized to it. Instead, I was sick for weeks. I also ignored warnings about the fifth-rate meat in Latin America. Not all of it tasted good, but with each meal eaten in cheap restaurants, I could spend more money on liquor. Stupid. I remembered all the ruthless-looking fricassees of god-knew-what I had bought from street stalls. There was no recollection of having seen a health inspection sticker anywhere.

Eating in Canada all my life led me to believe restaurant food was safe. I didn't care to change my thinking while on the road – even though the sketchy budget diners across South America had all but screamed out warnings to stay away. At the very least, the horsemeat I had unwittingly eaten in Cartagena should have tipped me off. And that was the single time I'd asked about the contents of my meal. It dawned on me that only a select number of cooks knew what was actually in the food I had eaten. Dammit! I should have been more careful. I thought back to the monkey I had chowed down on in Ecuador. Moaning, I recalled all my culinary adventures and indiscretions. The punishment seemed to fit the crime.

My neighbour's rasping cough shook me back into the moment. Glancing sideways, I could see the towel covering the woman's face, now doused with red. She quieted down and removed the cloth, showing her face. Drawn, thin and in her late 20s, a wraith of the woman's high cheek-boned good looks remained, not yet totally wasted by illness. Her half-opened eyes were bloodshot and it was difficult to read much from them, other than agony. The mouthful of still-polished teeth indicated she had taken care of herself, and her lips, although blood-stained, remained full. All the same, it didn't look like death would wait a week for her. Dropping my gaze before we made eye contact, I wondered what she must have been like in good health.

With another lung-shredding hack, the woman stuffed the bloody towel into her bag, pulling out a fresh one to cover her face. I could hear her kids dashing about the outer deck, not knowing whether they were trying to give their mom a break or if they were oblivious to her suffering. Either way, the woman's respite didn't last. The smallest child, shrieking, galloped past my hammock and collided with her. She wound up and smacked the little boy. The youngster burst into tears and ran away. Through her gurgling cough, the woman wept and I could hear her groaning,

"Ahh … Dios, Dios."

Pain seemed to close in on her from everywhere. I stared up at the chipped paint on the ceiling, and thought she must have undertaken the voyage to get the children to a place where they would be safe after she died – maybe she was bringing them to a relative? To a monastery? Wherever the trip ended, it would almost certainly be the woman's final destination. I shuddered, one cot over from the pall of death, mired in parasitic misery. At least I had the luxury of feeling tremendously sorry for myself, while the gagging woman put her children first. She soldiered on knowing she would die, while I wished the ship had a bar. Such strength set against my lack of moral character made me wonder if a fatal sickness of the body could be any worse than a terminally ill mind.

The sun set on the jungle, over a swath of river that must have been three miles wide. Dizzy from lack of food and sickness, I reflected on whether I was learning the lessons I hoped to be taught in South America. It was a question without answer and I drifted into a restless sleep. In my next waking moment, I was shoved from my hammock. The dark figure of a man holding a machine gun stood over top of me.

"Get up, gringo!"

Disoriented, I picked myself up from the deck and looked around. Passengers all over the boat grabbed their things and hurried down a gangplank.

"Move it! Let's go!" the soldier roared in thickly accented English.

He jammed his knee into the small of my back, obliging me to push my bike into a clearing in the midnight black of the jungle. Ten more armed men were aboard, harassing people. Three soldiers trained their weapons on the cargo hold while a fourth held a lantern. Two of the ship's crew moved everything from below decks: Banana bunches; sacks of rice; hogtied animals; and, reams of farm implements. I did not see the sick woman. I didn't hear her children either. But I had more pressing worries: The military man had business with me.

"What are you doing in this jungle, gringo?" he spat, rolling his 'r's. "Are you bringing gunss for the Shining Path guerrillass?"

"No."

"What about dope? You got some coca?"

"No, I don't."

"Don't tell me this. Any gringoss on this river are haffing gunss or dope. Which one are you? You say right now!"

"All I've got are clothes and bike tools in those bags. I can open them up." I moved to unzip one of the bags, but the soldier shook his head.

"It iss my job to keep people from making trouble on this river. You are smart gringo, yes? I think you can get safe to border. How much money iss with you?"

I swallowed hard, hoping he hadn't noticed the nervous gesture. My money belt held about $400 – the last of my cash – hidden beneath my shorts.

"I only took traveller's cheques. I can show you – in my bike bag."

"A lie! How did you pay to go on the boat?"

I hadn't paid yet, and told the soldier I had just enough Peruvian money left for the fare. I turned my pockets inside out, showing him the bit that remained after cashing my last cheque a week before. He shifted his gun from his shoulder strap with a deliberate, slow movement.

"I tol' you many gringoss are with the guerrillass. I haff arrested them on this river. We can keep you here for long. This iss even if you haff no gunss. Do you haff some more money? Maybe you like to stay here and think about this?"

The situation was deteriorating, with the possibility of it turning tragic. I advanced toward my panniers once again, where my empty traveller's chequebooks sat in a side pocket. I'd considered tossing them out, but after the robbery in El Salvador I thought it best to keep records in case my bags turned up some place without me. The cardboard envelope from the travel agency held a sheet of paper that bank tellers had marked with the date and location of each cheque cashed. The soldier didn't stop me this time as I reached for the envelope. Maybe he thought I was revealing my money stash. But it was just a prop for a story I hoped he would believe.

"Really, this is all I have – this and the money to pay for the ticket to the border. I'm supposed to have some cash wired to me at the Brazilian line – just enough for my visa and to get me to Manaus.

Once I'm there, I'll pick up some traveller's cheques that are waiting for me, a book of cheques just like this one. I don't have any other money."

I assumed that the soldier must know about money belts and would simply tear off my shorts to grab mine. But the shakedown continued.

"What else iss in this bag, gringo?"

"Like I said: clothes and bike tools. There are some books and a razor. That's about it."

"Show me these toolss."

The assortment of wrenches, screwdrivers and pliers was unimpressive. My dirty laundry also made an appearance. I hoped the tattered clothing would suggest a history of insolvent gutter travel. A final pull displayed an empty bag, devoid of any bank notes. The man with the machine gun shone a flashlight on my stuff.

"What iss in the other bag? More junk?"

I began to unravel the second pannier, removing some books.

"Stop! I do not haff time to see this garbage. If I hear of any gringoss down the river giving troubless, I will know it iss you! Go away."

By then the rest of the passengers had lined up to get back on board. I was grateful not to have been robbed again, but thoughts of that afternoon's horror show in the bathroom slithered back to mind. I returned to my place, trying to shake off the jitters when I noticed my neighbour's hammock was gone. There was no sign of either her or her three children. They must have gotten off at one of the whistle stops – surely I would have woken up in the commotion if she had died. Wouldn't her kids have cried loudly enough to shake me from sleep? My thoughts spun toward terrible conclusions. I fell into jarring dreams, waking up periodically, drenched in sweat and feeling awful.

At dawn, the smells of gruel and instant coffee wafted throughout the decks. I connected up with the jumble of passengers working their way to the galley as the boat pulled toward shore. Agitated, I scanned the docks for soldiers. Stopping felt like a waste of time, especially when there was no doctor on board. But this layover turned out to be worth it. Three more passengers plunked their bags onto the lower deck: two old men and a young woman travelling alone, her passport identifying her as Brazilian. And, lord, was she a welcome sight. She was the flawless Brazilian beauty I had heard so much about, her generous hips and breasts accentuated by the tight, cropped clothing then in vogue for South American ladies. She would have had no trouble strutting proudly in the latest and greatest from the most progressive bikini makers in Rio. The woman smiled and spun her glorious hourglass figure, twisting to slip past a man attending to a cage of chickens.

Such knee-jerk sexiness did not belong that deep in the jungle. I nearly spilled coffee down my shirt trying to figure out what she was doing there. Then I sat on my cot, brainstorming a plan to talk to her as she slung her hammock four spots down. I was nervous about attempting an approach in Spanish, and my Portuguese was limited to five or six phrases listed in a Brazilian travel guide. Desire moved achingly through me in ways I hadn't thought possible. The recent brush with the barmaid in Yurimaguas had stirred me; now the sight of the amazing woman with the coffee-coloured skin nearly drove me mad. My mind raced – I was ready for action. Or so I thought for a short moment. The language barrier possibly could be overcome, but the fact I was sick with parasites, broke, and living in a hammock on a boat was a problem. Still, I had to try something. Maybe she could speak English.

I resolved to walk past her, planning to make eye contact. After a string of mental pep talks, I stiffened and rose to move closer to the woman. The not-so-casual stroll accomplished nothing. She avoided looking in my direction, almost certainly by design; every traveller on the river checked me over at least once. I had been a conspicuous foreigner throughout Latin America. Now, this far downriver, I might as well have been from outer space. She knew I was there. She just didn't care.

Smarting over being ignored and feeling nauseous, I sulked in my hammock until the next morning. At long last, a whistle blew. The boat slowed toward the wharf at the Peruvian settlement of Santa Rosa for border procedures. Later, a short water taxi ride over to the Brazilian frontier town of Tabatinga raised my hopes of finding a doctor. But things hooked a sharp turn for the worse as I rolled my bike up to the pier. A goat had gotten loose in the crush of disembarking passengers, and its owner almost knocked me into the river trying to catch the bleating ungulate. Then a man carrying an outboard motor gouged my ribcage with the propeller. My abysmal state of mind boiled over when the inner tube squeezed out of my back tire and wrapped itself around the cog set, seizing the bike.

With the rage that always simmered close to the surface, I took decisive action, booting the spokes right off the back wheel. Bellowing, I condemned the front wheel to a similar fate. Hard kicks to the frame failed to bend it, but I did manage to snap the handlebars and tear off the gear cables. Embarrassment quickly replaced momentary satisfaction with the effort. A gathering of wide-eyed men stared from the dock as I unhooked my panniers from the now-defunct bicycle. I felt my face flush with red. Worse, as I took stock of my stunned audience, the woman with the hourglass figure stood only 20 feet from the action. She looked at me with an amused smile, lit a cigarette, and walked away.

Already off to a rotten start in Brazil, I couldn't find a doctor's office in small and dirty Tabatinga. There was one other alternative. Colombia's southernmost reach was visible across the river from Peru which, along with Brazil, formed a region known as the tri-border area. A short cab ride from Tabatinga took me to the nearby Colombian town, called Leticia – no border-crossing formalities required. Rushing through Leticia's business strip, my pulse quickened when I saw a medical office that looked open. I ran but, being in shockingly bad shape, I couldn't keep the pace. It was nearly four o'clock when I implored the receptionist for an appointment. The office was closing soon and the doctor wanted to get home for Christmas. Could I come back in two days, she asked, pointing to a calendar. Lacking the words to ask properly, I pressed my palms together in mock prayer, held my belly and pulled a mournful face.

The receptionist rolled her eyes, and said she'd see what she could do. Twenty minutes later I was shown into an office, where the doctor sat at a desk.

"What can I do for you?" he asked in English.

"Well, um, I have parasites."

"I see. What sort?"

"They're worms, but I'm not exactly sure what kind."

The doctor's face was scored with fatigue. But he patiently heard me out as I told the tale of the awful creature I'd pulled out of my ass.

"That's unfortunate, but I treat this sort of thing often. It's common among people who live in the area. I can't be completely certain what type of parasite you have, but it's likely one of two kinds. I'll prescribe two different courses of pills. They should clear up your problem. I will caution you against eating any more meat in the cities. The butchers there tend to use unsanitary practices."

The doctor had the necessary pills on hand. I thanked him profusely and did not quibble with the 40 dollar bill. Dry swallowing two tablets brought immense psychological relief. But it didn't last. The doctor had jotted down an English translation on how often to take the pills: twice a day for the first one, three times for the second, both for ten days. What would happen then? Would dead worms appear at bathroom visits – or would they somehow disintegrate inside me? I hoped for the latter, but if that were the case, how would I know if the medication had worked? Either way, I planned to get checked out back in Vancouver.

I straggled around Leticia for an hour, looking for a no-frills hotel. An overpriced room teemed with tiny brown lizards that crept in through a gap under the door. I didn't mind them, except for the ones that ran across my face as I tried to sleep. On Christmas morning, the desk clerk told me no ships sailed that day. I guessed that was a scheduling quirk rather than anything holiday-related, as most of Leticia's businesses were open and people carried on as though it were any other day. No Christmas lights adorned houses; no decorations hung anywhere and no tinny recordings of 'Feliz Navidad' blared from speakers. There weren't even any church bells. All that helped to temper a bout of homesickness; my family celebrates Christmas in a huge way and I was missing out. Dismissing the self-indulgent brooding, I walked down to the docks at Tabatinga to confirm an early sailing for Manaus.

The Brazilian boat was newer and snazzier than the Peruvian models. A crew in white uniforms mopped the decks and kept the bathrooms clean, the folksy stench of the previous voyages now swapped for an almost sterile feel. An irritating feature, however, was the stereo system. The five days to Manaus incorporated ear-splitting Latino pop with a wide selection of other appalling melodies. It got even louder at night when the planked area on the bow lit up and transformed into a mini-disco. The tepid, reggae-esque strains of UB40's 'Red Red Wine' and the nauseating staccato of the mega-hit 'Macarena' reverberated into the Amazon night. I hadn't heard the latter until after arriving in Latin America, and soon learned a day there was not complete unless the tune was played dozens of times at peak volume. It blared in the streets, on buses, and out of the windows of private homes. On the boat, it was inescapable.

Other than enduring that sonic onslaught and witnessing a creepy-looking turtle barbeque one afternoon, the trip to Manaus supplied little more than hammock-riding monotony. No time remained to explore the city when the boat docked. Nor was ducking out of Manaus any great loss – South America's cathedrals and plazas had long since blurred into an indistinct bore. The main thing was getting a bus north to Venezuela and from there, a plane to Miami. If any cash remained beyond a few dollars to tide me over in the States, I would surely get wasted.

My soul is lost, it's lost its way. It's been living in this lost highway.
— ANGRY SAMOANS

James motored across Texas as I drifted back through a night of getting thoroughly hammered at a hotel bar in Caracas. The bartender had set me up with rock bottom liquor all night, while cockroaches hummed throughout the place. They tyrannized the lounge and, when I got up in the morning still half-drunk, my bed crawled with the over-sized vermin. I remembered brushing them out of the sheets and trying vainly to get back to sleep. As foul as that wake-up call had been, freezing in the back of James' truck felt even worse than wallowing in roaches.

We had been rolling for two hours and I'd needed to pee almost as soon as we started moving. When James pulled over, Edward said we weren't far from Wichita Falls, which meant nothing to me. The younger brother double-timed it to a bush just big enough to conceal the fact he was urinating. James had stopped the truck in the parking lot of what looked like an abandoned fast food restaurant. I unzipped my pants in front of a weather-beaten plastic clown's face that had apparently once served as a drive-thru speaker.

"Thanks a lot! I really appreciate it, jerk!" the clown berated. The speaker in its mouth crackled forth the indignant protest of a female burger joint employee. She caught me off-guard and I pissed all over

159

my hands. A closer look revealed a clear sightline between the restaurant and the drive-thru order spot. The restaurant was indeed open for business – things were just a little slow. James and Edward had seen the entire piece of foolery and split their sides laughing as I wiped off my hands.

"Let's go!" I roared.

"I think there's still enough gas to get us all the way to Amarillo. Just bang on the window if you have to piss again!" James taunted.

The bastard's spirits had turned 180 degrees now that his brother was riding shotgun, and I envied those guys the rest of the way to Amarillo. James didn't stop again until he parked at a diner, four hours later. Kinked from the cold, I jumped out of the truck and hurried toward the smell of fried onions drifting from the swinging door. I didn't wait for James or Edward and nearly smacked into a Stetson-wearing cowpoke on the way inside. Adjusting from the pickup bed's dreary view to the fluorescent glow of the diner had a drug-like effect. A down-home waitress in an orange polyester uniform approached me.

"Are ya by yourself darlin'?"

The two jovial brothers walked in before I could answer.

Edward said, "He's our friend," and the waitress seated us right next to the buffet. James and Edward already had plates in their hands, and were raiding the chicken-steak-and-gravy section. I wasn't sure how they got ahead of me, but I vowed to make up for it by eating enough to stay full for three days. Breaded chicken breasts, mashed potatoes and gravy, turnip greens and biscuits slopped over my plate. Apple and chocolate pies sat, warming, at the end of the buffet. A general thaw worked its way through my bones as I gobbled the hot food.

"Slow down there, boy. There's plenty more where that came from! Heh-heh," Edward said, with his bowl-full-of-jelly laugh.

"I just wanna make sure I get my money's worth. The food's delicious and I bet there won't be anything this good outside of Texas."

James, always with the unwelcome practicalities, cut in.

"So what are you going to do after we eat?"

"Well, my plans haven't changed since Dallas. I suppose I'm in for more hitchhiking."

I still didn't know what the two brothers had planned in Amarillo, nor did I care, unless it involved a warm place to crash. But James' weird hospitality had almost reached its end.

"Okay. Well, we're headed into town, but I can drop you back at the highway if you want."

"Sounds great," I said, and again buried my face in biscuits and gravy. Edward tried to lighten things up when my short response stopped conversation at the table. The roly-poly Texan started telling Jeff Foxworthy's 'You might be a redneck' jokes. That was the first I'd ever heard of Foxworthy. His punch lines were only mildly amusing, though Edward's delivery may have lacked professional timing. A huge second helping, pie, coffee and a dozen redneck jokes later, the three of us stood at the cash register. James glowered at me with a slow shake of his head when Edward offered to pick up the tab.

"We'll all be paying for our own meals tonight. You also forgot to leave a tip."

I walked back to the table and laid down a dollar. It was nearly dark when James dropped me off at the edge of town. He looked like he wanted to salute me as he shook my hand and wished me well.

"I'm gonna drop off Edward and head to the drugstore to grab a few things. I'll circle back in an hour to see if you're still standing here."

Parting company with James left me with a strange feeling. The man took me 1,200 miles that he didn't have to, meaning that I'd covered more distance with him than anyone else in the past six months. I don't know how I would have survived the road if he hadn't picked me up; despite his temper, he was the sanest person I'd travelled with for any length of time. James' generosity probably saved me from having to endure a grab bag of short hops with any number of dangerous weirdos. I never figured out what made him so erratic, but it was irrelevant by then. Besides, I was as sick of him as I'm sure he was of me. Edward was all smiles as the Toyota roared back onto the highway. I found a good spot to stick out a thumb and I never saw James Tosca again.

The highway out of Amarillo was narrow compared with the behemoth Interstates I'd stumbled along in Florida. The place James dropped me at had the advantage of being next to a wide gravel shoulder, and plenty of light poured in from the city. Within 15 minutes, a woman pulled up in a blue Ford Taurus. No other woman had stopped to offer me a ride during those travels – a subject that came up as soon as I had set my panniers in the back seat.

"Hi I'm Terry. Look, I know it's weird for a girl to pick up a hitch-hiker, especially at night, but it looks so scary out there on that high-way. I thought you looked cold, so I stopped. My friends say I do this too much. I'm always hearing 'Terry, don't pick these guys up. Are you out of your mind? You could get killed!' But I like to do a good turn when I can, so don't hurt me, okay? I mean, I helped you – it just wouldn't be fair if you did something to me."

Terry's eyes were anxious.

"Hey, I'm thankful that you stopped for me. I'm just heading home. I'm not here to cause any trouble."

She snorted riotous laughter when I told her where I was going.

"I'm sorry – I might have made more problems for you than I solved. I'm only going a couple of miles, up to my daddy's ranch. I'm not sure how many cars'll pass by there."

That was bad news, but I didn't say anything about it to Terry. We stopped five minutes later and I stood in near total darkness on the roadside. I caught a break before starting to root around in the night for a place to pitch my tent. A junked Chevy blinked its lights as it drove toward me, stopping just off the deserted highway, 100 feet ahead. My heart beat faster as I opened the Chev's rusty door.

"Howdy!" came the greeting from inside. "Where ya headed?"

I realized then I would once again have to become accustomed to the scorn of Americans who thought of Canada as a 10,000-mile-

162

long hockey rink. Not having to retell the story continually was one advantage of travelling with James. When he stopped laughing, my new host told me his name was Lou. He said it wasn't his real name, but that's what everybody called him.

"Yep, they been callin' me Lou since the '60s. I'm jus' haulin' up to New Mexico t'see m'girlfriend. It's a good long ways I'm goin', maybe 200 miles. I can drop you off 'bout halfway between Santa Fe and Albuquerque near a place called Clines Corners."

Two hundred miles was far better than I'd hoped. The temperature had nose-dived in Amarillo and the idea of spending hours in a heated car held grand appeal. The scant light in the car showed Lou was in his 50s, grizzled and bearded, with a faded tattoo inked into his right forearm. A trampled, brown cowboy hat rested evenly on top of his head and black coils of hair spilled out in all directions. Lou looked like he'd been a beer-drinking roustabout since the days of the 75 cent six-pack.

"Do you live in Texas?" I asked him.

"Some of the time. It depends what kinda mood the old lady's in, y'know? I got a spread about 30 miles outside of Amarillo that I share with my brother. That's where I'm comin' from now. Me an' him's always fightin' about the place. Our daddy left it to us when he died back in '86. But I tell ya, that brother of mine, he won't do any upkeep. When I'm around I'm always cuttin' and haulin' and makin' repairs. Then I go off to see the ol' lady for a while and when I come back it's all fucked up again. I dunno. If things work out on this visit, maybe I'll stay and just ask 'im to buy me out, not that he's likely to have enough money to do it, but even at a bargain price, I could be shut of him. But aw hell, I've been sayin' the same damn thing for years now, heh heh."

"Does your girlfriend have a nice place?"

"Naw, it's kind of a shithole and I'm always hearin' about it from her, too. I'm never there long enough to fix up the porch – and the kitchen floor's saggin'. It's her fault I don't stay on longer. I mean, dammit, can't a man relax some before his ol' lady's got a hammer an' saw in his hands? There's some stuff I should be attendin' to, like the five or six dead cars in her front yard. Most of 'em are mine, it's true. An' they don't pretty up the place much but it's like I keep tellin' her – I'm gonna fix 'em up and sell 'em off for cash money. I'm a mechanic, y'see. I'll tell ya what, though, I can feel it – this time it's gonna be all right between us. What about you? You got a sweetie?"

There was no one. My last girlfriend had dumped me for a cute lesbian. It was still something of a sore spot, but the story was unusual and I'd told it to select audiences in recent months, though not to James. Talking about it helped and I figured Lou would get a charge out of the tale.

"Well, my most recent girlfriend was a dominatrix who went both ways."

"What in hell?"

"Yeah, it's kinda weird, but it was the coolest three months of my life. We met at a club in Vancouver that was having a sadomasochistic party. I had no idea what the scene was about, but let me tell you, man, some of those leather and rubber outfits that the chicks had on were enough to send a guy into orbit. I mean we're talking low cut here. There was all sorts of other stuff going on that wasn't my thing: people wearing spiked dog collars leading others around on leashes; fat guys in G-strings. I didn't really know what to do at this place, but there was this hot girl in a snug leather outfit who was whipping people, and I sorta thought, okay I'll go for this. So she's got me tied up to a metal post and I've taken my shirt off and she lets go with the whip. It didn't hurt though, I mean not really and – "

"Shee-it boy! Are you tryin' to tell me you let her crack you with a bullwhip?"

Lou's tone was playful but incredulous.

"Yeah, well, it was a new thing. She was gorgeous and I was trying to figure out the scene."

"Ha ha! That's a good one! You took off your shirt and allowed her

164

to give you a beating? Oh shit, that's somethin' I never heard about before! Haw! Well I hope you got a little nookie from her."

"Well, not exactly. The whipping didn't last long and there were some other guys in line, so I moved on. But I'd noticed this other gal watching the whole thing. Man, she was something! All done out in super-tight leather pants and a very revealing rubber top. We sorta bumped into each other a bunch of times at the club and I hoped I wasn't imagining that we had a vibe going on. We kinda smiled at each other as we watched a circus freak shove a purple neon tube down his throat and his tummy glowed out purple. Anyway, I just said hi and asked her for her number. I couldn't believe my luck when it was the right number."

"Sonuvabitch boy! That sounds like one hell of a party you two was at. Then what'd you do?"

"We just met for a date. She told me right up front she was into women as well as men, and she liked to keep her options open there. It also turns out that she's a dominatrix. I didn't quite know what that was, but she reminded me about the whipping I had taken at the club on the weekend. She said she did that kind of thing professionally and really liked to hurt people when she hit them with the leather."

"Dammit boy, I'm tellin' you I would have run screaming from that one! Whoo-wee! So did you let her beat on ya too?"

"No. I mean yes. Well, not right away. We went out a few times and she tried some things on me in her dungeon, or 'dungeonette', as she called it. It was the craziest place I'd ever seen – full of whips and chains, mirrors, rubber sheets and even a set of manacles to hang guys from the ceiling. She's got a long list of clients, and makes enough money using that stuff to pay her bills. I thought that was pretty weird, and I wasn't sure I could hang out with her. But her line of work is different from prostitution. People actually pay her big cash to have her beat them into a sort of sexual ecstasy – sometimes until they bleed – without touching her. As balls-out wacky as that sounded, I didn't understand how truly bizarre the whole thing was until she took me to the next S&M bash."

"Another party, huh?"

"Yeah, and Lou, I tell ya I'd never imagined such crazy shit. The setup was an old warehouse downtown that somebody had laid out as an art gallery – an industrial joint with super-high ceilings. The first thing I saw when we walked in was a naked guy who had been strapped to a cross with layers of plastic wrap. The thing was rigged up to a pulley, and somebody hoisted him to the top of the 40-foot ceiling. They left him there all night, dry humping this cross."

"Sumbitch! That crew'll be earnin' their way to the heat in the hereafter! Dang!"

"Yeah, well then there was a guy in a pair of lederhosen–"

"What the hell?"

"You know, those short leather pants you see pictures of people wearing at Octoberfest?"

"Yeah, all right. I know what you mean."

"Anyway, this guy was wearing a pair of those things, but they were down around his ankles. Some chick was flogging his balls with a riding crop and a crowd of people chanted stuff and insulted the guy. But the riding crop chick meant business; I mean she was really laying into this dude. She hit him so many times I thought she would cut him to bits. The guy loved it, though. He was really into pain and humiliation, I guess. I'd barely gotten in the door when all this was going on. But it was a big warehouse and the weirdest shit was happening at the back – "

"Waitaminit! What was your girlfriend doing while all this was happening?"

"I saw her spanking some people and making out with two other women. She'd gone to the party topless, with red lipstick on her nipples. Every lesbian in the place was drooling over her."

"Weren't the men looking her up an' down, too?"

"I don't know if there were any straight guys there."

"Shee-it! So you just let all this go on?"

166

"What choice did I have? It was her thing, and I liked having a dominatrix for a girlfriend – kinda subversive."

"I'da never stood for such goin's on. But you said somethin' about the real crazy stuff happenin' at the back?"

"Yeah, it was fucked up! There was a guy wearing a scuba-diving suit and a gas mask, with a bunch of springs hooking the suit onto a metal frame. The guy also had on high heels that barely touched the floor, and he sorta just hung there. All of a sudden, he shot straight upward and writhed in pain. I could hear him screaming from under the gas mask. When he stopped shrieking he went all limber and loose, with the heels just kinda bouncing off the ground. I had no idea what had happened – I just stared at the guy. A minute later, he screamed again and he did this whole twisting and bouncing thing. Finally, I asked this woman next to me what was going on. She said the guy on the jolly jumper had electrodes attached to both his nipples, his dick and up his ass. A drag queen over to the side controlled the electricity with a switch and jolted the guy every few minutes. Man, I laughed! But she looked at me all pissed off, and told me the whole thing was 'sexual art' and that there was nothing funny about it. I couldn't believe people took that shit seriously."

Lou said nothing, his eyes riveted to the road. I wondered if I'd gone too far in mentioning the last part. All the things I had just talked about were still relatively new and unusual to me – and I came from the city. How much stranger must it have been for an older man from the country, probably set in his ways? It was uncomfortably quiet in Lou's car for the next ten minutes.

"So what happened to the guy with the electrodes?" Lou finally asked.

"I'm not sure. I didn't see him again."

"Man, that's a tellin' I won't soon forget. Sounds like you had some wild times – not sure it's a trip I'd wanna take, though! Then again, maybe it could be fun. I might jus' ask the ol' lady about that. Heh heh. Man, I wish I had a big ol' doobie to puff right now. You got anything to smoke?"

"No man. A joint would be far out though."

"Yeah, it sure would. But I dunno, I kinda lay off of the stuff for a while after my pet monkey died. See, I had him at my spread in Texas. He belonged to me and m'brother. He was a cute little sucker – we named him Gary after a dog we had when we was kids. Anyway, Gary was about the only thing me an' m'brother agreed about. We loved him and we let him roam all over the place. We couldn't house break 'im so we put 'im in diapers. Yep, the two of us never fought about that. If anything, we fought to take turns changing 'im. Heh heh. Yeah, Gary would swing from the ceiling lamps and get into just about everything. We'd near to bust a gut laughin'! Oh man, we'd get high and watch that monkey scoot everywhere. But, y'know, he was smart too. He'd go outside to play on the clothesline or in the trees, but he never went too far and always knew when to come in for supper. Well, shit, one night we got real stoned, set to watchin' some TV and we forgot about 'im. Damn, wasn't it a cold winter night and we went out callin' 'im, 'Gary, Gary!' But he didn't come. We was out with flashlights for an hour before we found 'im froze to death in the big ol' ash tree right next to the window he came in through sometimes. Shit. All of it 'cause we got too damned high. That was a little over a year back, and I've only smoked a couple times since then 'cause I still feel bad about losing my monkey."

I told Lou I was sorry about Gary. It was sad to lose a monkey. We cruised on through the night for two more hours, talking easily. Lou pulled over at a truck stop in New Mexico where a road shoots north toward Santa Fe, forking off the Albuquerque Interstate route. He shook my hand and wished me luck. I was going to need it because it was bloody cold.

I moved a ways out from the truck stop to find a place to pitch my tent. At first, I thought the cold cut so deep because I'd just gotten out of Lou's car. But the tent spikes bent when I tried to drive them into the desert sand. The ground was frozen solid. I had to put up the tent with no pegs to hold it down. Spreading out inside was like lying on top of a sheet of ice. I rifled through my panniers and pulled out every shred of clothing, put all of it on and slipped inside my meagre sleeping bag. I lay awake, teeth chattering, listening to the odd semi-truck rumbling off in the distance toward Santa Fe or Albuquerque.

The night passed in unbearable cold. Exhaustion pulled me to sleep once or twice, but mere minutes would pass before the raw chill woke me up again. It didn't make sense – I was still pretty far south, in the desert no less. How could it be this bitter? I would have to make some inquiries. When the highway traffic got louder, I removed two layers of clothing and struck the tent. It was still dark when I trudged in the direction of the truck stop. The thermometer at the top of the gas station's marquee read minus twenty-two.

I tried to shake off the temperature, when I saw a man having an even worse night than the one I had just spent. He was lying on a bench outside the truck stop, with a cowboy hat shielding his face. The guy had only a single layer of clothing and a sleeveless vest to stave off the elements. He didn't budge as I stalked past.

Inside, the place was deserted except for the cashier, who eyed me up sharply. The receptions I had become used to when travelling with James and the one I got walking in alone with bike bags at five in the morning were markedly different. Nevertheless, I treasured the minutes inside that truck stop. My body shook from its core as I poured steaming coffee into the biggest Styrofoam cup on the counter. I had taken to drinking it black because it stayed hotter that way, though I fidgeted with cream and sugar packets to stall for time.

"It's a cold one out there, eh?"

The cashier, a woman in her 50s or 60s with her grey hair in a bun, peered at me through drugstore-rack glasses and said nothing. There would be no chatting in the store to warm up. I moved slowly toward the register with my coffee – a bargain at 69 cents for a large cup. My hand shook violently as I parted with the loose change and grabbed the key to the bathroom.

Cascades of hot water from the faucet burned my hands, and

169

I glanced up at a horrible sight in the mirror. The arctic night had turned my face completely red except for my nose, which had mutated into a purplish lump. I wondered if I wasn't frostbitten. Too stiff from a night of lying on top of the frozen desert, a full-on trucker shower and change of clothes was not going to happen. Instead, I lathered streams of liquid soap into my hands, rubbing the bubbly potion into my face. Ten minutes of this warmed me up, though the shivering had not yet abated.

The cashier sneered in my direction as I headed outside, back to the mad world of Interstates and unforgettable drivers. A pink sun had just begun to glow in the east, traffic had picked up, and the edge of the parking lot made for a promising spot to stick out a thumb. Grateful the previous night's chicken steak dinner still partially filled my belly, I sipped the coffee, thinking the day was off to a decent beginning.

Less than an hour passed before a guy in an aged and sorry Ford stopped to pick me up. He was Mexican and spoke little English, but I understood that he was from Chihuahua State, just over the border. I asked him about the temperature – I'd retained the word 'frio:' Spanish for 'cold.' He said Chihuahua got cold, and sometimes it even snowed. I'd never heard of snow in Mexico before. The car conked out as I considered this, and the driver smiled wanly, jumping out to fool around under the hood. Ten minutes later, we were rolling again but advanced only two miles before the car sagged into another bout of engine failure. More tinkering with the motor ensued, followed by a short gain on the highway and another breakdown. I wished him "buena suerte," before hiking over the next rise in the road as he tried to cajole the last miles from his dying beast.

Slogging past the spiked agave plants and patches of creosote bush, I thought about the way time fluctuates on the road. When you're cruising, it's a fast go. Remaining stuck on the side of a highway stretches out the hours. Weather affects road time, too: On a sunny and warm day, the first hour spent waiting for a lift is only marginally longer than sixty minutes of riding; the next hour of sitting tight eats up more time than the last; and, so on. In biting cold or a driving rain, time grinds along just like it does working a boring job, the critical difference being that a shift at mind-numbing employment is usually relieved after eight or so hours. No such guarantees exist on the road.

I listened to a Budweiser truck and a length of cars, figuring out how the sounds of vehicles also play tricks. The high-pitched whine of a passing car is much different from the low chugging noises of a vehicle slowing down. A long wait can fool a hitchhiker into hearing a car 'stop' after it passes, when it has actually continued down the highway. Sustained roadside delays sometimes slow approaching vehicles to the hitcher's eye. The mind wills a driver to decelerate, and actually believes the car is braking, though the speed never changes and the phantom ride blazes past. A day on the periphery will turn those kinds of mirages into heartbreak.

That morning all of those elements colluded to throw me into a highway time warp. The hours crept by without a ride, long after I'd finished my coffee. Sometime that afternoon, a beefy pickup truck with a winch on the front bumper pulled over. I wanted to click my frozen heels as I chased after it. A welcome surprise greeted me as I hopped in. The driver was black – the first black person to pick me up in 2,000 miles of travel. I had agonized over the racist obloquy I'd heard along the way. Not having spoken against it weighed heavily on my conscience. Now a live target of that prejudice sat in the driver's seat, offering me a ride. I hoped I didn't look too dumbfounded as I extended my hand. The man's name was Reg – another former Air Force guy, on his way to Albuquerque.

"I was stationed there during my flying days, after I got back from Vietnam. I'm originally from L.A. but I liked the area and I decided to stay after 24 years in the service. I'm always driving from one part of the state to another, but you're the first hitchhiker I've seen in probably a year. I'm headed into town to pick up some supplies for my ranch, but I'm gonna be early, so I can show you around for a while if you like."

171

That sounded immeasurably better than waiting for another ride. I knew I'd have to get back to that soon enough, but there was no hurry. I told Reg I'd love to see the place. I also figured he'd know why it felt like the North Pole out there.

"Why is it so damned cold? I mean, I know it's January, but aren't we in a desert here – a desert in the southern half of the United States?"

Reg, muscular and bearded, grinned in a way that comes only from a man who has learned by painful experience.

"It's colder than it normally is this time of year. But you're in the high plains, man – we're not far from the Rockies. I thought the same thing as you about the desert until I got stuck in an unheated hangar my first winter here. Shoot, for a guy from L.A., New Mexico seemed like a real bad fit. I tell you what, though; leaving L.A. was the best move I ever could have made. I really love the wide-open terrain, and the air here is so much cleaner than that smog in California. Yeah, it sure does get cold, but it's good for my health. I dunno, I was in Vietnam for a little over a year and the humidity there was more than I could take. I stayed in L.A. for three months after my tour; when I signed up again, they sent me to Albuquerque and I never looked back."

Reg drove west, and had no questions for me as the flat, sandy ground gave way to rolling hills. He was relaxed and had no need to peer at the details of a younger man trying to get home. But I had more to ask him.

"Something's really bothered me since getting to the States – all the white people who spout racist crap. I mean, yeah, we've got our share of racists in Canada, but it's more open and more vicious here – almost like its second nature to some people in this country. What's that like for you? Do you ever get the shitty end of it?"

Reg said nothing. His facial expression quickly changed from one of calm to a steel grimace. Uneasy minutes ticked by before he answered.

172

"Look, as an ex-serviceman, I mostly get respect. But I still hear people talk when they think I don't hear. I've come to a place where I'm okay with things – I've done the best I can in this life and nobody – and I mean nobody – can take that away from me with bigotry."

Reg spoke with tempered anger. I had obviously pried a door he hadn't imagined would be opened.

"But if people will talk like that within earshot, there must still be a bigger problem in this country than your own success can cut through."

"What are you talking about?"

"You've done pretty well for yourself even though fucked-up attitudes must have worked against you. As far as I can tell, those ways of thinking are still there in the worst way. How big is the problem and what can be done about it?"

More silence. I really had a way of mucking things up socially. Reg shifted tensely, and took his time before answering.

"Let me tell you something about racism in this country. In 1970, a locomotive pulled up two blocks from my cousin's house in Compton. The engine detached itself and left behind two boxcars. The cars were locked but left unguarded – in that part of town, it wasn't long before they got jimmied open. What do you think was inside – keeping in mind it was an almost all-black neighbourhood?"

"No idea."

"Guns and dope. It was a pretty clear message: 'G'wan black man – go and kill yourself!' And that was only five years after the Watts riots. I guess the powers that be decided the job wasn't finished yet. And look at the record in that neighbourhood since then: Gang violence and drug use are in the stratosphere. People are still poor, but they're worse off now, and the violence is spilling outside the gangs. Witness the Rodney King riots a few years back," Reg said, his tone impassioned.

Now it was my turn to sit quietly. The boxcar set-up sounded like a plotline for a movie, or an urban legend. But Reg was no dummy and I didn't think he would be fooled by a made-up story. Maybe he was trying to sell me a bridge for asking stupid questions.

"Who dropped the boxcars there?"

"Who do you think? There sure wasn't any forwarding address or any bills of lading to go by. It had to have been the government."

"Couldn't it have been gangsters getting their wires crossed, moving stuff around?"

"That's not what people in the neighbourhood said. Nobody staked a claim to it. It was just a free-for-all for whoever was on the spot."

Reg concluded his telling as the Sandia Mountains rose in the distance. Thirty minutes later, we were in downtown Albuquerque, Reg naming the commercial towers in a subdued tone. We swung out toward the old quarter's colonial-era structures and flat-topped adobe houses. Then we turned to cross the dry bed of the Rio Grande, Reg dropping me off well before he was to make his business connection. He'd had enough of my questions.

I hunched against the cold on the open road, and a short hop took me to a town whose name I can't remember. Sleep-deprived and grumpy the next morning, I exhaled in dejection at the sight of another hitchhiker standing on the best hitchhiking spot. This was the first competition I'd encountered in all my American travels. The possibility of a rivalry had occurred to me, but I'd seen very few others on the highway. There was the frozen guy James picked up in the Florida panhandle, but I could recall having seen only two or three more. Vying for a spot with a fellow hitcher now struck me as ridiculous.

But there could be no jousting for position. Hitchhiking code ordained that, as second comer, I had to find another place. I planned to engage him in brief conversation and move on.

"Good morning," I said, approaching from behind.

"Well hullo!" the man said, turning on his heels in surprise. "How's it going? It sure is a nice day, isn't it? Wow, what a day and what a crazy night last night! I'm still a little drunk but boom-boom-a-boom! I'm gonna have more fun today!"

The dude was a lisping, gay American Indian. He wore filthy, torn jeans, had greasy long hair and a crazy smile on his face. He clutched a garbage bag containing some belongings, and held a full bottle of beer in a pocket torn into the lining of his jean jacket. The short and pudgy fellow surged with excitement about the day.

"I'm going to San Francisco! I can't wait! I hear it's so much fun and the parties are like, boom-boom-boom! What about you? Where are you going?"

I squelched a laugh as he wiggled his hips describing the San Francisco parties, and told him that I'd been thinking about the Grand Canyon. My Arizona map marked it about 50 miles north of Interstate 40 as the highway closed in on the California state line. Lying in my tent the night before, I began to harbour the unlikely hope that just the right ride would pick me up once I got to Arizona, take me to the canyon, and detour back to the Interstate.

"Oh, I hate the Grand Canyon. It's such a drag. It's no fun at all, and the tourists? Puh-leeze! Oh heavens, if I were you I'd just head straight home. Don't give that silly canyon another thought."

I said I'd take that under advisement, and asked him how easy it was to hitchhike in the area.

"Oh! You're hitchhiking too? Well, how about that! I think this is a pretty good spot but I'll just go down the road a ways. That way it's not such a big deal if somebody comes – they'll see only one guy, instead of two. It's hard to get rides in pairs, you know. I've just stood for days sometimes when I'm travelling with another guy. And I'm telling you – no ifs, ands or buts – there's no kind of drag like that kind of drag. Well, b'bye. Oh, if somebody picks you up first and I'm still standing down the road, have them pick me up too, okay? This should work out just great!"

I wished the little party animal safe travels and watched him mince down the highway, wondering why he was backing off. It should have been me getting gone. Then I understood: He thought he had to move on. He was probably afraid of me. I shook my head in shame.

Icy gusts ripped down that deserted stretch of highway the entire morning before things changed in a hurry. I'm not sure how long I stood there shivering before the huge yellow car pulled over. It was an amazing car – 20 feet of sleek Detroit rolling stock. This thing was massive! With glee at my luck, I opened the door and tossed my gear into the back of the ancient Cadillac. I learned the name of its owner before I could open my mouth.

"I'm Mr. Yellowhorse! And this is my fuckin' car! Welcome, white boy. Sit down and enjoy the ride. Where the fuck ya goin'?"

Two men were perched in the front seat. One sat at the wheel without making a sound. The other, Mr. Yellowhorse, announced they were Indians – Navajo, he later explained. He wore a ten-gallon cowboy hat with a plume stuck in the hatband. He had long, braided hair, huge mirror sunglasses and a tan leather jacket with tassels. Mr. Yellowhorse looked absolutely awesome.

"I said where the fuck ya goin'?"

Mr. Yellowhorse whistled when I explained. Then he took a long gulp from a bottle of Smirnoff Vodka he apparently had been working on for some time. I was glad he was not driving.

"Look man, I say I'm Mr. Yellowhorse and I own everything you see outside this car. And I already told you I own this fuckin' car too. About the only thing you can see that I don't own is my cousin Sully here. But he's at the wheel, so he's my driver in my car on my land. You got that?"

"Got it, Mr. Yellowhorse."

"Get some r'spect in that tone of voice when you talk to me, boy. You don't sound like you got enough 'spect for me. I'll tell you something. Not only do I own this car and this land, I own all the businesses too. Lookathere!"

The Cadillac accelerated past an emporium marked with the name Yellowhorse.

"Now, what does that fuckin' sign say?"

"It says Yellowhorse."

176

"Lookahere Sully! We got us a reg'lar Einstein white boy back there! Look over there – another Yellowhorse business. You gettin' the picture about whose place you're in?"

"I think so, Mr. Yellowhorse."

"I think so, Mr. Yellowhorse," he mocked in a nasally tone. "I know you think I'm up to no good but I got proof about this. Look here."

Mr. Yellowhorse retrieved a bulging wallet from his back pocket, and pulled out a driver's licence. I tugged on it, thinking he wanted me to check out the particulars.

"Don't you try to steal my driver's licence, punk! You think I'm not wise to your thieving ways, white boy? I know what's on your mind."

"I wasn't trying to steal anything."

Sully remained quiet while Mr. Yellowhorse indulged in another long pull on his bottle of Smirnoff. He sized me up in the rear-view mirror.

"You look pretty skinny. You not eatin' so well?"

I fumbled an explanation that I was working from a strict budget.

"So you're broke, are you? You get in my car on my land with no fuckin' money, do you? Well, I'll tell you something. I'm not the kinda guy who lets people leave my property in worse shape than they got here in. Here, take this."

Mr. Yellowhorse pulled out a ten-dollar bill and handed it to me.

"I'm a successful Navajo man and I make good fuckin' money. Have a bit of it, white boy, and don't let no one ever say the Indian never did nothin' for you. Here, have a drink too."

Mr. Yellowhorse passed his bottle backward and I gulped enthusiastically. I contemplated a second drink, but Mr. Yellowhorse snapped his fingers to indicate that I was finished. The vodka roiled my empty stomach and blazed straight to my head. Stupefied, I gazed at the newly acquired bill for a minute before putting it away.

"Hey, thanks Mr. Yellowhorse," I said.

But my gratitude fell on deaf ears. My hosts were pointing and speaking in Navajo. Sully stopped the car for another hitchhiker. It was the little guy on his way to San Francisco.

"Hey! It's you again! Wow, who'd have thought it? This is great!" he said heaving himself and his torn green garbage bag into the cavernous back seat.

He said his name was Wendell, and began talking to Mr. Yellowhorse in the Navajo tongue. I had never heard it spoken before that day; it sounded like a rushing river. Meantime, Sully pulled us onto a badly paved road that ran parallel to Interstate 40. This was the old Route 66 that the new highway had replaced years before. It was mostly out of service, but commerce still prospered along parts of the famous old thoroughfare. Sully stopped at a used car dealership and got out. He said nothing, but Mr. Yellowhorse told us we still had another hour to go.

While Sully ran his errand, the conversation between the two Navajo speakers became heated, and Wendell was getting upset. I suspected Mr. Yellowhorse was picking on him for being gay. They squabbled until Sully returned to drive us back down Route 66.

"Hey white boy, here, have another drink. But don't give any to that bitch."

I swigged back a torrent of vodka. Craning over with a fearful glance at the rear-view mirror, Wendell reached his hand toward me behind the seat. At the very least, I thought I owed it to him to risk the fury of Mr. Yellowhorse. Even settling into a well-oiled state, I still felt lousy about taking Wendell's spot earlier on. I attempted a surreptitious pass.

"I said don't give any to that bitch! Gimme that back!"

With a deferent shrug to Wendell, I sent the bottle forward. Then he and Mr. Yellowhorse resumed their bickering. The argument sustained the flowing river sound at first, but quickly lost it. Mr. Yellowhorse shouted and Wendell nearly burst into tears. Sully stopped the car and Wendell jumped out, waddling furiously down Route 66. Mr. Yellowhorse had something else to get off his chest.

"You wanted to fuck that bitch, didn't you?"

"I did not," I said, shocked out of my Smirnoff buzz.

"Yes you did! You wanted to fuck that bitch hard!"

Sully snorted a nose laugh and pressed the enormous car onward. I stewed wordlessly. He ditched the old road to make better time on the Interstate, eventually turning toward a small settlement a quarter-mile off the highway. I cast a glance down the Interstate for a good place to resume thumbing as the Cadillac drove down a dirt road lined with sagebrush and cholla cacti. They stopped at a strip of property where a barbed wire fence penned in a flock of sheep, and a massive rock face shrouded the land in a winter shadow.

One last ride that afternoon took me just over the Arizona line. Another night tenting, unremarkable except for the stabbing cold, passed into dawn. A short lift in the morning moved me through the desert wastes and left me quaking next to a cactus. A coyote eyed me up warily as it scurried across the highway. I watched tumbleweeds blow across the road for five hours before an outlandish camper van pulled over. The contraption had begun its days as a flatbed truck, but since had been remodelled. Bolted to the deck was a parti-coloured camper with warped panelling. A concatenation of ill-fitting braces held the thing snug to the back of the cab, but way off-centre and listing heavily to one side. That the vehicle hadn't been ticketed off the road struck me as peculiar. Groaning, I prepared to meet yet another freak at the wheel.

"Hey man. Hop in. I'm Dave. I've been driving all day here and I was looking for some company. You look frozen through. Here, I'll crank up the heat."

"Yeah, it's chilly out there. How far are you going?"

"I'm headed to San Diego to see my boyfriend. I left St. Louis yesterday. Man, it's a long drive."

Dave wore an obsolete brown shrub of a moustache. It handle-barred in swishing chunks down either side of his mouth and his hair was unkempt. The effect was a slightly awry Freddie Mercury affectation; Dave's mop needed a trim to nail the '70s party boy look. His jeans and t-shirt could have been part of anyone's outfit except that both were tightly drawn over his body. Dave thrust his pelvis forward and leaned back on the deep benchseat, revealing a prominent bulge in his trousers.

"Are you a fun guy?" Dave wanted to know. "I'm thinking of stopping for some beer whenever I pull over tonight."

I was road-weary and did not feel like dealing with this. In an ill-advised move, I delivered my liberal-attitude-toward-gays homily.

"Look Dave, I think gayness is cool. I've got all sorts of gay friends in Vancouver, which is where I'm heading by the way, but I'm straight. I'm open-minded and all that. And I've done my share of sexual experimentation, but I've satisfied my curiosity and – "

"Curiosity? What have you been curious about?"

"Nothing that concerns you, that's definite."

"Have you ever been with a man?"

"No. Like I said, I'm straight."

"But if you're curious sexually and you've never been with a man, how do you know it's not for you?"

"Some things, you just know."

"I don't believe that. Nobody is totally straight – nobody. I'll tell you something else: I took two U-turns to get back to you. I've never picked up a hitchhiker before, but you looked so fucking hot there on the roadside, I just had to go back. I know what it's like to be curious, and I know I'm filthy as hell but I've got the camper back there. We could spend the night togeth–"

"No thanks! I'm not having sex with you. Understand that."

"Can I touch your penis then?"

"No! Fuck man!"

"Why not, I mean there's a big difference between having sex and me just grabbing your dick. Damn, I mean you can even leave your pants on. I'll just rub it and we'll see what happens."

"No."

"Don't be such a downer. I mean once I get to San Diego, I'm stuck

180

with my boyfriend. He's a great guy, but I really need some other cock before I'm on monogamy duty for six weeks."

"Dave, I don't care about that. I mean c'mon, look at what you're saying here. There's no way this is going to happen. Be realistic."

"I am being realistic. This is my van and I reserve the right to fuck whoever rides in it – or at least try to. Relax. I really want us to get it on. Think about it – my camper is nice and warm and the two of us could just – "

"DAVE! Cool it! I said no."

"You need to loosen up. I bet you would if we had some beer. I'm definitely getting some once we're in California. You'll tranq out a bit then."

"Whatever. I'm not, under any circumstances, going to do any-thing remotely sexual with you whether drunk, sober or even if I die and reincarnate as a homo."

"Aha! So you do have gay thoughts! I knew it – you've thought about being gay in another life! Well man, let's not wait until you're reborn. I'm gonna grab your dick right now!" Dave said raising his hand.

This was getting out of control. I moved as far over as I could.

"The hell you are. I'm sorrier about the way I phrased that than you can possibly imagine. Dammit. NO, NO and fucking NO!"

"Oh horseshit. Look, how about this. Just let me see your penis, okay? I promise I won't touch it – Mr. 'I'm not gay.' I'll just look at it and then I'll show you mine, all right? Then we'll see who's not gay."

"My parts stay in my pants. That's final."

"Nothing's final until we get some beer into you. We'll see who's not drunk and buns-up naked in my camper toni-i-i-i-ight!" Dave said in a singsong voice.

Burying my head in my hands, I sighed, trying to make sense of my predicament. Dave was going all the way to California, but he was also a lunatic. I figured beating the hell out of him wouldn't be a problem if he tried to force himself. Of course, there were all sorts of things I didn't know. Did he have a gun? Or maybe he was some sort of martial arts expert. The first was plausible, the second unlikely. What about the camper – closed off from the cab – were there other freaks back there? That idea scared me. But I was willing to bet Dave was just a horny asshole, not a dangerous one. Besides, a 'safe' ride all the way to California, plus the possibility of beer, were enticing. I decided to hang tough.

"What's on your mind? Does it have to do with penises?"

"I am not thinking about penises."

Dave chuckled. "I bet you are. I can always tell when a guy's thinking about cock."

Dave's persistence was a drag.

"Fucking shut up, Dave. I'm really tired and you pushing me is gonna make me snap in a minute. It takes a lot of antagonizing to get me throwing punches, but let me tell you, señor, you're pretty close. So do us both a favour and DROP IT!"

"Oh yeah, 'señor?' You better not try anything because I'll drive us straight on into traffic and kill us both. I don't give a fuck! You're not the only one in this van who can be dangerous, you know. So you cool it unless you want to die!"

We had the beginnings of an understanding. Other than Dave's hyperventilation, we drove on silently past the distant mesas and buttes. It was 45 minutes before Dave spoke.

"Look, I guess if you haven't tried anything crazy by now, you're probably all right. I'll put away the cock-talk. Let's just stop for a burger. We can tranq out over some beers later on."

I agreed to the truce and we stopped for Whoppers and fries near Holbrook. Dave brought in a roadmap to plan his route; he wanted to get to Barstow that night. I thought about beer, wondering how many I'd be able to knock back before things got crazy. Back on the road, heading west, the hitchhikers proliferated. Most of them were grubby and spent-looking. Dave pulled over for the cleanest one. A blond, slightly rotund guy turned to see the tilted, whack-o-van idling on the shoulder. He picked up his bag and trundled toward us.

"Hey, thanks for stopping," said the newcomer as he plopped down on the bench seat, moving me into the middle. "I'm Joe."

Dave was especially direct.

"I'm Dave and I'm going to San Diego to see my boyfriend. I stopped because I thought you were hot. I thought this guy was hot too," he said, jabbing a thumb in my direction, "but he says he's not interested in ass-fucking. What about you, Joe? Are you into fooling around?"

I hung my head. Poor Joe, he hadn't been in the van even a minute.

"Uh, no – thanks. I'm just on my way to Vegas to get some work with a roofing company. Look, I'll bail right now, if that's a problem."

"No, it's no problem. I just find it funny that I do you guys the favour of picking you up and nobody wants to give up a little dick. No, no problem at all. Look, I'm going to grab some beer once we get to Barstow. I just hope you tight-asses loosen up at Miller Time."

Joe flushed with embarrassment and moaned in disbelief. He said nothing else, apparently hoping his original answer would stand. I tried to change the subject with some questions about the roofing job, but Dave wasn't having it.

"Hello-o-o! Um, I'm the one driving here and I sure don't give a shit about working on houses in Las Vegas. So I don't want to hear any more about it. In fact, all I really want to know about is your cocks. How big are you, Joe?"

"None of your business," Joe uttered, stunned.

"The hell it's not. Your cock is in my van. That makes it my business. So come on, what are talking about here? Six inches, eight inches – ten?"

The blush returned to Joe's face but he said nothing. Dave glanced sideways at me.

"I can only bet you won't tell me anything about your schlong either. Or maybe you've changed your mind?"

I shot back an angry glare, and a heavy silence persisted for hours. Signs at the California State boundary indicated that drivers had to declare whether they carried any non-indigenous fruits or vegetables.

"Neither of you guys've got any fruits or any shit you're not supposed to have, do you?" Dave demanded. "I don't need any trouble here."

Joe and I shook our heads. Another two hours passed with minimal chatter before we pulled over at a massive truck stop in Barstow. I jumped out of the cab to stretch my legs. The parking lot was cold and dark, and Dave strode the length of a neighbouring semi-trailer. He worked to convince Joe and me that he'd undergone a change of heart.

"Look, I've got two bunks in the camper – a big one and a little one. You guys can share the big one up top and I'll take the smaller one. And no, you don't have to fuck me. I was just trying to get a little. I mean, hey, you can't blame me for trying."

Dave showed us the bunks and said he'd be right back with some beer. Alone with Joe for the first time, I explained myself.

"Look man, I'm just trying to get home; a few beers to take the edge off is all I'm looking for here. I don't know what you're thinking, but a warm bed for the night would be great. All I wanna do is sleep. If that moron tries anything, I'll punch him in the head. How are you seeing this?"

Joe was 30ish, with a quiet voice. He had twiddled uncomfortably during the ride, saying almost nothing. There in the parking lot he spoke the longest I'd yet heard from him.

"I'm in this for the beers, too. I was thinking about jumping out back in Arizona where there's a smaller road that cuts up to Vegas. But there's way less traffic and the beers sounded pretty good. I'm with you – we'll split that bunk. Any funny business with that guy and we'll have to shit-kick him."

I nodded and thought about safe haven. I had a phone number for my sister's former best friend, Rochelle, who lived in Los Angeles.

184

She and I had made indefinite plans for me to stop and see her on my way back to Vancouver. The trouble was that relations between the two friends had hit the rocks when Rochelle abandoned my sister during a recent crisis. But my sister hadn't written her off entirely, and I hoped to grab a shower and a hot meal at Rochelle's apartment.

I was even thinking about asking her to lend me 20 bucks, when Dave returned with 24 cans of cold Budweiser, plunking them down on the floor and motioning that we should dig in. The call could wait. Frosty suds slid down my throat and my problems dissolved. Somehow, Dave wasn't even acting like a jerk; at least, he refrained from talking about penises, though I was sure that wouldn't last. I plunged into my second brew minutes later, which made Dave beam lasciviously. Damn, I thought, I'd need six more beers before I could face his crap again. I stood up and explained that I needed to find a phone booth.

I walked to one at the other end of the lot and dialed collect to Los Angeles.

"Thanks for taking the call. I'm in Barstow. I was thinking about hitching to town for a visit."

"You want to come all that way to see me?"

The complex tone of Rochelle's voice indicated that this was a no-go, likely for a number of reasons. She said that she and her boyfriend had barely seen each other in weeks. Work and school ate up all their time. Social engagements spanned their calendar, "we need to spend a weekend alone together." I tried a tactical shift, hoping a dire account of my fortunes might sway her.

"Yeah, I had to head back after my teaching gig in Colombia fell through, so I took a roundabout route to Miami and I've been hitch-hiking ever since."

Rochelle went on about her busy, L.A. lifestyle.

"...so it's been a lot of go-go-go without a break. It's too bad it won't work out this time but it'd be great to see you back in Vancouver some time soon."

I said goodbye and footslogged back to the camper for another beer. Not finding shelter in L.A. was a blow. It wouldn't have gotten me any closer to home, but momentary refuge from the frigid Interstate would have been welcome. I had been counting on it since starting out in Miami. Fairly speaking, however, the cold shoulder was not the complete measure of Rochelle's character. Years before she had pulled me out of serious trouble, taking me to her house when I was drunk and the cops were breaking up a near-riot I had helped start.

Semi-trailers manoeuvred through the parking lot as I approached the van. Dave would almost certainly be up to some sort of mayhem by now. Sure enough, the back door was locked. I rattled the handle persistently before Dave, heaving with exasperation, barged through the doorway. Joe had seated himself at the back of the camper, and looked relieved at my arrival.

"I thought you were going somewhere," Dave snapped.

"Yeah, I had to make a phone call. Now I'm back. Pass me a beer?"

Dave scowled and Joe got up to find a bathroom.

"Look you asshole," said Dave, "Joe was digging my shit. I mean I was working it with him and if you had just stayed away, I'd be getting fucked right now."

"I kinda doubt that, Dave. Joe told me he is definitely not partial to your scene. I'm pretty sure he's straight so you're wasting your time," I said casually, cracking a beer.

Dave had had a couple of beers himself, reinvigorating his drive.

"That's what you think! Like I said before, nobody is totally straight – least of all that guy. I'm pretty sure he just hasn't met the right queer. I'm a horny bastard, so I'm definitely the right guy to get him in touch with his gay side. And I'd appreciate you not putting words in his mouth – the only thing I want going into his mouth is me!"

The evening with Dave dwindled perilously close to its end. I figured on hanging out for two more beers. Then it would be time to split. I drank and said nothing, but Dave was back in hot pursuit.

"Look, I know we got off on the wrong foot earlier but now that we've had a few drinks and a chance to relax, maybe I could just take a look at your balls 'n' ass?"

"No Dave."

"Aw c'mon – please?"

"Nope."

"Fuck man, I think I've totally gone over the top with the hospitality thing: a ride, beer and a place to sleep. All I want is bit of fucktime, I mean, let's go man – it's ass o'clock. I either want to see that sweet bum of yours or rub dicks together."

Joe returned just in time to keep me from flipping out, throwing an already taut situation into freeze-frame. Dave glared at me, then at Joe before storming outside. Joe sat down, helping himself to a Bud.

"What was going on there?"

"Just more crap from Dave. He figured he'd about lured you into the sack with his fruity moustache and camper van boudoir. I told him that he had you all wrong. Then he took another crack at me."

"Damn, that guy's a freak. Well listen, I've got some weed. Do you smoke?"

"Ah, Joe! A joint would be awesome right now! Something of an after-dinner mint for our liquid supper."

"Got any rolling papers?"

"No," I told him. "I'll get some, though."

"Okay, I'll stay here and break up some of these buds," he said producing a small, plastic baggie. "You see what you can rustle up. Most of these truck stop places don't sell papers. But if no one else has any, go to the counter and buy a pouch of loose tobacco. Some brands put a pack of rollies inside."

Definitely, bumming the papers would be preferable to buying them, but there were difficulties with that. Essentially, the dangers were two-fold: If you found someone carrying rollies and they gave you one or two, they could justify tagging along for a toke; the second problem cropped up if you asked the wrong person. I'd gotten hostile rebukes before. A guy even threatened to call the cops on me. That had only happened one time but it left a strong impression. It paid to be careful – I had been busted for a joint once when I was 17. The cops strip-searched me and I spent the day in jail.

Unable to work up the nerve to ask a trucker, I parted with two bucks for the tobacco and all-important papers. Spending the money stressed me out, but I looked forward to getting high. Joe twisted two small piles of weed into joints, and the clouds of dope smoke settled my head. Dave stayed away – we had no idea where. The two of us drank his beer and smoked some more, relaxing in the warm camper. Joe told me he was recently divorced, and leaving a small town in Arizona to start fresh in Vegas. The roofing gig was just money for the time being – he mostly worked in framing and hoped to get back into that soon. We talked until Dave all but wrenched the door off its hinges, assailing our sanctuary and grinning malevolently.

"Okay, you guys have to go sit up front for a while."

Dave was up to something evil.

"Why?" I asked.

"Just get in the cab, you two."

"Dave, if I'm going to do something, I want to know why – what's going on?" I pressed.

"Okay, you asked – see this guy? This is Ricky!"

Dave thrust a pathetic shade of a human being into the doorway.

"He's all high on crank and he wants to get it on. So while me and this wild man rock the house, you guys are going to have to excuse us."

Ricky was an addict. Covered with bad tattoos that bore the hallmarks of jailhouse artistry, his grey skin recalled a failed embalming job. He was gaunt and his teeth had rotted to the gums. Scabs oozed all over his face. The dude was probably in his 20s, but could have been mistaken for a 90-year-old drunk.

"Let's go, you guys! You're not playing the game! Me and sweetie-pants here need to get our rocks off and we haven't got all night, so c'mon," Dave shouted.

188

Joe and I gawked. The addict flashed us a deathly glare. I had noticed a handful of filthy ghosts like this one at truck stops along the way. Was this how they got by? Appalled and fascinated, I couldn't believe this was about to happen. Without another word, Joe and I grabbed a six-pack and made the trip to the cab. As soon as we took our spots in the front seat, the van began to sway. Then it shook. Then we heard ungodly noises.

"Aaaaarrrrrgggghhhh!"

Joe and I drank in a stupor.

"AAAARRRGGGHHHH!"

I had to say something.

"Can you believe these dickheads? This is fucked up."

"Look," said Joe, "I don't know where Dave went when he was gone for those couple of hours but let's hope both of them split when they're finished. I hate the idea of being in this guy's truck, but it's better than sleeping outside. Like we said, if he tries anything, we'll stick together."

Joe had the right idea about compromises and alliances on the road. As the rollicking in the back hit a climax, my thoughts shifted to worries about any cops who might see the tottering van. But neither of us finished a whole beer before the creaking camper door announced somebody's departure. Dave strolled over with a Budweiser in his hand, grinning like an asshole.

"We're done! You can go and sit back there if you want. Ricky says he knows where some more party boys are hanging out, so we'll just take our time. I'll see you two later – but don't think for one minute I've stopped thinking about getting some hard cock from you guys!"

It had been a long, long day. Joe and I drank one more beer apiece before taking the upper bunk. I crashed into a deep separation from consciousness that wasn't to last long. An hour or so passed before Dave returned, slamming the door behind him. He had Ricky in one hand and a bottle of whisky in the other.

"Get up and get out! I'm not getting any cock around here, so you two private dicks are gonna have to fuck off. I'm going to San Diego tonight and Ricky is going to make sure I get there happy!"

Still drunk, I could barely lift my head. Craning my neck toward the floor, I took in the sight of the two men. Dave shuffled his feet and drank. Ricky, awful to behold, fondled Dave's crotch.

"C'mon, let's shake it, fellas! It's a long drive to Southern California. Out out out!"

I roused myself from the warm camper bed, now comprehending the turn of events.

"Man, you are one lucky son of a bitch. I'll tell you what, Dave: If I were a violent guy, I'd beat you silly. You said we could sleep here – "

"Hey, sorry man, but it shouldn't be a surprise that I'm doing this. I told you the whole time we should be fucking. You kept turning me down and then you screwed up my chances with Joe. Why should I let you guys have a freebie stay in my camper if you won't even let me give you a blowjob? I mean shit...."

Joe said nothing. Dave apologized again, saying he'd try to find us a ride on his CB radio. I told him to piss off. Joe and I walked aimlessly across the frozen parking lot. We covered four hundred feet before he spoke up.

"I know how we can stay warm tonight. This is a pretty big truck stop. The newer ones this size have movie theatres in 'em. They're free for truck drivers. Hitchhikers aren't supposed to go inside, but if you're quiet nobody will throw you out."

Hallelujah! If Joe was right, my nights of frozen tenting were over. I wanted to hug him. Instead, we walked past some truckers who milled about the lobby, talking about the road. Hunger gnawed as the tantalizing smell of hot beef sandwiches emanated from the diner. Joe pointed toward a long hallway and a sign that read "Movie Theatre – Truck Drivers Only." Joe might have passed for a trucker with his protruding belly, beer shirt and ill-fitting jeans. I followed him closely.

The theatre was packed with long haulers; the smell of popcorn filled the air and junk littered the floor. I settled into a padded seat and saw that the movie was about the singer Tina Turner. Still newly awake and feeling the strong effects of beer and weed, I soon became engrossed in the plot. A tense sequence depicted Turner's husband beating her up. In the next aisle, an older trucker was outraged.

"Look at this garbage – this damn junglebunny beating up his wife. This country has gone to shit with everything the coloureds are doing. Look at all the crime everywhere in America and look who's doin' it!"

Nobody responded. One thing I had noticed along the way was that most truckers were white. I couldn't tell who was in the theatre, but I guessed there were no black drivers taking in the movie. Before I could think any more, Joe shook me awake.

"Hey man, it's six o'clock in the morning. They're about to do a shift change and I heard the janitors talking. I think they're gonna call the cops on us for trespassing. We have to get out of here fast."

Hung over and exhausted, I trailed Joe by a step. We crossed the highway and sat down behind a warehouse to figure out directions. Joe generously fired up his last joint. After we smoked, the prospect of hitting the freeway struck me as less daunting than it had at first light. Nevertheless, I scrupled over something Joe had mentioned the night before. He had absolutely no cash. I was hardly flush – not even 15 dollars remained in my wallet – but I handed him three one-dollar bills.

"Thanks man. This should get me some toast and coffee anyway. Well, I guess I'm heading over that way for Vegas traffic. Good luck getting home."

All of a sudden I absolutely did not feel like spending the day hitchhiking. I regretted giving Joe only three bucks; slipping him one of the fives would have been better. He probably thought I was a cheap bastard. I chewed over the miserly gesture for half an hour until a guy in a checked suit and a fedora pulled over in his K-Car. The dude was in his 60s, headed to Bakersfield for a Sunday church service. He preached about picking up hitchhikers as part of his duty in "God's army," but if I tried to rob him, he'd "bop me in the nose." Whatever. I was stoned and mumbled a thank-you. At least he kept the lecture short and didn't try to hand me any copies of The Watchtower. He dropped me off at an exit just outside the city.

That morning I reached a new stage of fatigue and hunger. Worrisome thoughts held sway: While I had done my best to put it out of mind, I remained unsure about the effect of the Colombian doctor's medicine. The obscenity on the Amazonian boat had not repeated itself, but I was thinner than I had ever been. I hoped that was only because I hadn't eaten much in recent weeks. Three famished hours later a semi-driver pulled over. His name was Stephen.

"I'm hauling this load to Sacramento. I can take you all the way there."

"Hey right on – I could sure use a long ride. Man, this hitchhiking is taking it out of me."

"Yeah, I see guys like you on the road all the time. It looks pretty rough out there. We're not supposed to because of the insurance, but I pick people up – especially when the weather is bad – just to get a guy out of the rain. It's also good to have someone to talk to."

"Well, I sure do appreciate it. It's good to be where it's warm and heading towards home."

Stephen had driven a few minutes when to my right, I saw something that needed explaining. Jammed into a valley two miles across and at least that deep were thousands and thousands of cows. As far as I could see, cattle stretched into the tapering distance of the valley. I could barely make out a blade of grass among them.

"What in hell are all those cows there for?"

"That's dinner for the eastern seaboard, man. In a week, they'll all be hamburgers at McDonald's in New York, Philadelphia and Detroit. I've moved 'em lots of times."

Stephen and I talked some more, and he offered me a Camel before lighting one. The thickset, balding trucker told me he had spent time in Vietnam: three extended tours with the army. The muscles

192

around his eyes began to twitch when he spoke of it. Most ex-soldiers equivocated or changed the subject when I sifted for details about the war. But Stephen had mentioned it himself, so I asked where he served and what he did. He said, "all over" and "killin' Cong." The questions brought about another of the tense moments I had a singular magic for creating.

Stephen twitched and smoked and drove without another word for 15 minutes. Then his eyes bulged and the muscles at the sockets trembled.

"Do you see that?" he demanded.

"What?"

"The dog. The fucking DOG!"

"Yeah, I see him," I replied meekly.

Stephen shook. His face reddened.

"Do you know what kind of dog that is?"

"Uh, a schnauzer?"

"It's a fucking FREEWAY dog! I've got 14 of 'em at home. People just get tired of looking after their dogs and dump 'em on the road to die. Do you know what I'd do if I caught somebody abandoning their dog on the freeway?"

I shook my head in fear as Stephen reached under his seat. He pulled out the largest handgun I had ever seen.

"I'd shoot 'em in the fuckin' head!"

He breathed laboriously. A demented frown dug deeply into his forehead. He did not replace the gun under his seat. Instead, he drove with both hands, two fingers pressing the weapon onto the steering wheel, in full view of anyone cruising the opposite direction. Freaked out to the point of wanting to leap from the moving truck, I congratulated myself for not being a negligent dog owner. I said nothing, but let out a long exhale when, some time after the outburst, Stephen needed the full use of both hands to shift gears and he tucked away the gun.

I fell asleep for what must have been three hours. It was dark when I woke up and Stephen was calm. In spite of the gun interlude, I felt bad for crashing out. The hitchhiker canon is staunch about not sleeping during a ride – it's just rude. I apologized and he told me we were still two hours out of Sacramento.

As Stephen geared down to pilot through the capital, I found myself ogling trucker's grills. When he stopped at one, I jumped to the ground, eager to find out whether the joint had a movie hut; discovery of the 'Highway Hilton' chain of all-night theatres made me feel like an experienced road warrior. The Sacramento truck stop did have a movie house, but it was smaller than the one in Barstow. A block-letter sign that said "No Hitchhikers" hung above the doorway. The place was crowded and my entrance turned some heads. The film hadn't started yet and drivers still chatted. I spied a place close to the front and picked my way through the tight rows, clenching my panniers.

"Where are you going there, pal?" an obese trucker wearing a Coors ball cap inquired.

"To that seat over there."

"You sure as shootin' don't look like a truck driver. Are you driving?"

"He ain't driving shit. I saw him jump out the passenger side of a rig ten minutes ago with them bags," called a voice from the back. "Why don't you hit the road? This place is for drivers, not freeloaders."

"Yeah, can't you read the sign? Take a hike," boomed a baritone order.

A murmur rose from rest of the 20 or so drivers and I left, disheartened. The theatre was a comfy place: The chairs were overstuffed and the room smelled of popcorn. Retreating to my tent, I found the night warmer than those spent on the high plateau. But the honking and revving traffic, coupled with my earlier nap in Stephen's truck, made sure I stayed awake. I was back on the road at the break of day.

A patchwork of rides took me all the way into the mountains near

Redding, California. One lift came with an old man who breathed through an oxygen tank. He drove a truck with Wyoming plates.

"I stopped for ya because I saw ya was white."

Dismay finally turned to anger.

"Look, I don't want to hear about colour. I'm sick of it. I hear it every day in this country. I can't wait to get back to Canada where most of the racists know enough to keep their mouths shut."

The white-haired driver knitted his eyebrows and gave his head a condescending shake.

"You're a guest in America, so you prob'ly don't know how bad the nigger problem is here," he wheezed. "Shoot, the only time I ever picked one up hitchhikin', I got robbed."

"I'm sorry to hear that, but the colour of the guy who robbed you doesn't mean anything."

The Wyomingite grimaced.

"The hell it don't! All them niggers think about is how to rob the white man. My cousin got a gun shoved in his face by a coon when he was in L.A. He was only there two days and the blacks are robbin' him. You don't hear about white men robbin' other white men – always the damn blacks."

"Oh come on – all kinds of people do stick-ups and muggings. I don't get where race comes into it."

"Maybe in Canada it's like that, but not here. The niggers in this country just want to sell dope and run around with guns."

"That's not true. There are movies and TV reports that portray that image – "

"'Cuz it is true! Dammit, how can you tell me I wasn't robbed by a black man with a gun?"

"It could just as easily have been a white guy who ripped you off."

"Uh-uh. Like I said, my cousin got robbed by a black guy and I've heard about others too – read about it in the newspaper."

"But the media picks which stories it'll print. Taking advantage of a race divide or inventing one sells newspapers."

"It don't change the fact the guy who took my money was black! I gotta watch out for myself and I'll say the same thing to any nigger who crosses my path."

I wanted to smack him.

"With an attitude like yours, it's no wonder you got robbed. I'd be pissed off, too. What'd you tell the guy? Be a good negro and don't pull a gun on me?"

"I didn't say nothin' of the kind! I asked him where he was goin' and before I know it, he's pulled out a gun. I stopped the truck and gave him my wallet. He took off runnin'. Far as I know the police never got him."

"So the guy got your cash – is it so hard just to call it bad luck and move on? You can't honestly believe all black people are like that guy."

"There probably are some decent black folks. But how am I supposed to tell 'em apart from the ones with guns? Far as I'm concerned, a nigger's a nigger."

We drove for five more minutes before he pulled over at his turn off, and I slammed the door getting out. I had learned to speak my mind on that score, but my conscience still was not at peace. I didn't demand he stop the truck. He didn't change his tune either. I was still fuming when the next ride materialized. A two-seater sports car with a glass hatchback skidded to a stop. The driver was apparently having trouble negotiating the thin layer of snow, which had begun to accumulate on the mountain highway over the previous hour. The passenger side door popped open and a woman's voice invited me inside.

"Get in! We haven't got all day here."

She stuck her acid-wash denim clad leg out of the car, leaning forward so I could climb into the back.

"C'mon! There's room for you and your stuff back there – let's go!"

Tucking one bag behind each seat and contorting into a fetal position, I jammed myself onto the rear dashboard. That provided me with an intimate view of the back of the driver's head. When I crooked my elbow, I could prop myself up for a better look at the

196

road. But the driver yelled that he couldn't see anything in the rear-view mirror – I would have to turn around and put my legs where my head was. The switch proved nearly impossible, with my knees dealing knocks to both skulls in front of me. Just as I settled into my new position, the car cranked into a higher gear, almost launching me into the front seat.

"Woo-hoo! Hold on tight there, hitchhiker! Ha ha! You're in for a harsh ride today! I'm Doug and I'll be your driver! This is my girl-friend, Cathy, and she'll be your co-pilot. The forecast is for snow, but that doesn't count for a rat's ass. We'll have you to wherever the hell you're going in no time. Where are you going, by the way?"

I told them and the customary laughter cackled from up front, though it carried on for an unnaturally long stretch. Unable to get much of a read on Doug or Cathy from the backseat, I didn't begin to worry until I craned my neck to see that each of them held an open bottle of beer. An empty case sat on the floor in front of me, which, when I got in, I had assumed was from some earlier date. Between the two seats, I saw another open case at Cathy's feet. It was two o'clock in the afternoon and the indicators were they had been drinking all day.

A nerve-shattering horn blast split the air as a semi-trailer jut-ted around the car, wobbling perilously into the next lane. Doug had weaved into the right-hand lane without looking or recognizing he had done so, cutting directly in front of the truck. The trailer, now passing us, continued to sway alarmingly before eventually settling down. In a moment, the truck picked up speed and disappeared. The horn threw me into a state of hyper-alertness and, looking into the rear-view mirror, I could see the colour had drained from my face.

"I can't believe people on this fuckin' road! This crappy driving's been goin' on all day. None of these goddamn truckers can drive any more," Cathy said.

"Damn straight, they can't. But I sure as fuck can! Watch this shit!"

Doug hit the gas and tore ahead, closing the gap on a pickup truck. Only three feet separated the sports car from the truck's rear bumper before Doug tried to pull into the next lane. But he yanked the steering wheel too hard and took us too far to the left. A car on that side braked to avoid a collision, slowing too quickly for the slick conditions and nearly skidded off the road. Watching those seconds unfold in the rear-view mirror charged me with terror.

"Fuck yeah, Doug! That was sweet! Ha ha ha ha! Let's do that shit again!"

"Maybe we could just slow down a bit, eh?" I implored. "That was pretty scary just now."

"Scary?" Doug asked. "You mean to say you were scared? Let me tell you something, Mr. Hitchhiker, that was nothing. I mean that wasn't even worth getting out of bed for. Tell 'im Cathy."

"Yeah, Doug pulls wicked stunts all the time. He's the best fuckin' driver in the state – or at least in Northern California."

"The whole damn state, Cathy, and you know it! Maybe the best in the country," Doug corrected.

"Yeah, you're right – at least the best in the state – so you just watch what you say. Besides, we bitched on the freeway for you."

"You what?" I asked.

Doug explained.

"We fuckin' U-turned back there just to pick you up, so don't complain about the ride. You do look a little scared, though. Here. Have a beer."

Keeping one hand on the steering wheel, Doug ducked to the floor on Cathy's side where the beer sat. The car sped crazily as he encountered Cathy's crotch.

"Hey! Keep your nose out of there! Hee hee! We can get to that later, Doug. Just get him a beer and get back to driving."

Doug did not look up at the road for way too long. Oncoming motorists would have seen an accelerating sportscar, apparently without a driver.

"Here ya go, man. Damn, you do look pale. What the hell's your problem? I toldja I'm the best damn driver there is."

"No, uh, I'm not worried about anything. I just need a beer, like, to cool out. No sweat at all. Um, I don't suppose you two are planning to stop any time soon, eh? I'm just about bursting back here."

"Nope. We stopped for beer a couple hours before we picked you up. We can't waste any time here. There's a bar way up ahead we're trying to get to in time to meet my uncle. So you have to hold it until we get there."

Doug had slowed the car to explain the plan. We still occupied the fast lane and the train of vehicles that had stacked up behind us started passing on the right. Somebody honked at us from a car I couldn't quite see.

"Holy bullshit! That fucker has some set of stones to lay on his horn at me. Whaddya think, Cathy? Do we run him down?"

"You know the answer to that, baby! Go get 'im! It's a good day to die! Us or him, it don't matter a shit!"

Without checking that he was clear, Doug jetted into the middle lane, inspiring another horn blast from behind.

"Hey man, whoa! That was too close! Maybe look at the mirror when you change lanes next time. And let's lay off the talk about dying!"

"Shut up!" Cathy screamed.

"I'm gonna tell you one time only, dude: Never tell me how to drive or you'll be fuckin' sorry. I really hate scaredy-cats. So just relax and we'll be all right."

Doug zigzagged across the lanes, eliciting a symphony of honks, Cathy responding to each one with a hearty, "Fuck You!"

The snow picked up as the pursuit continued and I wondered whether the sports car had winter tires. I doubted it and took mild amusement that it had even crossed my mind. Three dangerous passes later, Doug closed in on a Mazda. This was, presumably, the offending car. My heart pounded as Doug launched into his assault.

"Take that, asshole!" Doug yelled, nearly sideswiping the Mazda. Completing the pass, he swerved in front of the car, tapping the brakes. "That'll freak 'im out, make 'im think we're gonna stop right in front of 'im! This is beautiful!"

The Mazda pulled into the next lane, but Doug stayed ahead of the other driver, again braking slightly. The car's headlights flashed on and off, but Doug wouldn't let it pass. The Mazda even attempted a number of fakes and slow-downs to shake us off, without success. Other drivers saw the action and shot up ahead through the far lane. I wondered where the hell the cops were.

Hooting a "Yee-haw!" and cracking open a fresh beer, Doug proclaimed victory, only letting the Mazda squeeze by after keeping it at bay for ten minutes. Doug was now drinking quickly, and having a difficult time keeping a straight line. The sports car fishtailed into this lane and swerved into that one and back again, apparently creating the illusion that other cars were cutting in front of us. Ever vigilant, Cathy demanded action.

"Shit Doug, these fuckers keep cutting you off! Lookit that bastard there – he keeps moving into our lane. I'm gonna let those cocksuckers know not to fuck with us. Gimme some gas, baby!"

Doug stomped the pedal to the floor, nearly removing the sideview mirror from a station wagon in the left lane. I bit my lips into a painful mash as Cathy leaned way out her window and threw a full beer at a car 15 feet ahead. She missed and reached back for another bottle. Holding onto the frame of the hatchback with her left hand, she let the beer fly from her right. This one connected with the rear quarter panel.

"How do you like that, MutherFUCKER?" she screamed.

The other driver kept his window closed and I could see him shaking his head in disbelief. But Cathy wasn't done yet. She fired three or four more bottles, taking out a tail light with one of them. Cathy hollered and squealed in perverse delight, but Doug intervened.

"Hey, hey, nice job baby. But c'mon, we can't throw all our beers at people on the road, shit."

200

Cathy laughed and nodded in agreement, then screeched for Doug to stop.

"Doug, Doug, look at that river! What a gorgeous park! And the sign says you can get food there. I feel like an Oh Henry. Aw, let's stop for a minute baby, we can go for a walk by the river and have a couple beers – relax a little? This highway is fun but it's starting to get to me."

Doug grunted his approval and hit the brakes. Jerking us into the exit lane and gouging the car on a cement divider, he slid into the turnoff road and wobbled into the parking lot. I murmured a quiet prayer of gratitude when the engine had been cut. Doug all but fell out of the car, and Cathy slammed the passenger side door in my face as I tried to follow her out.

"Oops, sorry man. You all right? I hope I didn't get you there."

I told her I couldn't be better and stumbled away, overjoyed at being alive. A young Marine pulled over just before dark, on his way to a relative's house south of Seattle. I could ride with him the whole nine hours if I wanted. The next morning I stood in the pouring rain with my thumb out, 100 miles from home. Four solid lanes of traffic steamed ahead, continually slopping dirty water on me. I stood on that spot for an hour. Then another ticked past. Minutes into the third hour, a car pulled off the highway.

It was a pair of cops, intent on giving me a first-class takedown. One of them told me to put my hands on the hood of the car, slowly. He patted me down, demanded my ID and interrogated me, while the other one radioed in my passport info. I panicked when they shoved me into the back of the car. So close to home and getting busted? It was too grim to believe. But they cut me a break: If I could give them an address, they wouldn't lock me up. I mumbled that I knew some people at a truck stop and they dropped me at the closest one, with a warning to stay off the road.

Soaked and drinking black coffee, I pondered the depressing fact that I had one dollar in my pocket. I saw no other option but to head right back to the highway. The only thing left was to stand and will a ride to happen. Rain pelted for hours. Nobody stopped. Mind and body became numb. In the early afternoon, another cop signalled off the highway. This guy was friendlier than the other two had been. Dispatch told him it had been only a few hours since they moved me off the road. He would drive me back to the truck stop, but this was my last chance before the sheriff would throw me in jail for a week.

The threat of lockup forced me to run through the list of people in Vancouver I could call collect. Anyone in my family would have driven the three hours to come and grab me, but I'd resolved not to trouble them again after they replaced my gear following the robbery in El Salvador. More importantly, I wanted to conceal my desperation from them. Most of my friends had nine-to-five jobs and wouldn't be around until much later. I decided to phone my ex-girlfriend – the dominatrix. For once that day, luck was on my side; she was home to take the call and said she'd be down as fast as she could. She showed up around five-thirty, gave me a big hug and took me to a pizza restaurant in Seattle for one of the best meals I've ever eaten. I told stories and my ex filled me in on what was new in the world of sadomasochism. She was on the outs with her girlfriend, and I wondered if she had completely scratched men from her list. I knew I would ask her about that some time during the ride back to Vancouver.

POSTSCRIPT

Today is the greatest day I have ever known.
– SMASHING PUMPKINS

The sex farm, or Atlantis commune as it was known in the far-flung mountains, turned out not to be a good time. I found that out the hard way, after a two-day ramble from Bogotá. The road out of the Colombian capital rose steeply before plunging straight down the Andes. It gushed rain that afternoon and slashing torrents pounded my face. The rain had kicked me out of my languor in the past and, as darkness fell, blood pistoned through my body with new-found energy.

The road dropped even more sharply as the blackness became complete. I rode faster, and my panniers, poorly balanced, threw the bike off-centre. But I refused to touch the brake levers – maximum speed was vital. Water ran all over my body and a mad howl ripped from my lungs as thunder and lightning shook the uplands: Blasting through the Andean tempest tore a gaping chasm in life's outer limits. Even so, my poisoned spirit was not resurrected. The alcoholic excesses of Bogotá were close behind and I could not cut free from the most plaguing thoughts. I needed to blaze down that mountainside faster than the hellhounds could follow. Just then, incredibly, a flashlight beamed from the side of the road. A guy ran at me, shouting an insult:"¡Hijo de puta!"

Leaping at the chance to take leave of my mind altogether, I slammed on the brakes. My ridiculous bike fishtailed to a stop, nearly catapulting me face-first into the road. I ran screaming back up the hill. Ripping off his shirt and dropping his flashlight, the guy clenched his fists and yelled again, "¡Hijo de puta!"

Still 50 feet away, not breaking my sprint, I warned him, "I'm gonna fucking kill you!"

He stood there, rooted in the darkness until our eyes locked. Then, starting from a flatfooted stance, he took off at a hard sprint. I closed the gap, shrieking insanely. The chase lasted only about 200 feet. Mercifully, he was faster than I was and got away. Winded after the pursuit, I walked slowly back to my bike, sanity gradually returning.

I felt cleansed, more alive than I could ever remember, but minutes after the stillborn fight, my front tire blew. It wasn't just the tube – the entire rubber sidewall exploded and all my spares were gone. I thought of a fix. The paperback cover from my guidebook would serve as the missing part of the tire. It pained me to tear up a perfectly good book, but it was the only thing at hand.

The cardboard actually worked. I cruised farther down the mountain, lowering the speed in case the tire blew again. In just under half an hour, I reached a small town at the valley bottom, and almost shelled out for a hotel when a guy approached me to talk. He said a bus heading toward the far mountains would hit a crossroads about eight miles down the highway in two hours. Such a ride would be no problem if the tire held. It did not. It blew again just as the village lights faded behind me. I jerry-rigged another book cover fix-it and hurried on.

A dimly lit shelter at the side of the highway took shape out of the night, and the bus arrived more than an hour late. A curious feature of many of the Colombian buses, as of this one, was the artwork on the door separating the driver's cabin from the main length of the vehicle. The door unfolded when it closed, revealing an airbrushed painting of Christ with his bloody crown of thorns, eyes turned heavenward. The cartoon's forsaken stare made me laugh as the bus ground its way up the mountainside through the darkness.

The bus stopped in a medium-sized town, with the Atlantis commune still farther up the mountain. There were no transports until later the next day, so I took a room and poked around in the morning, looking for a replacement tire. I found one, but headed to a bar and drank beer instead of adjusting it to the wheel. There would be lots of time later to switch out the old tire. I had drunk my way toward a decent buzz by the time the bus rolled out, easing worries about the rickety thing negotiating the complicated mountain passes that reportedly lay ahead.

Decades had passed under the wheels of that ride – a school bus of 1930s vintage with patches of sheet metal riveted to the outer body, giving it an unhealthy, piebald look. I felt fortunate in my ignorance of mechanical workings. An automotive mind no doubt would have cringed at the thought of travelling in such a jalopy. The one thing I did find appealing was the creative use of the roof. A month's production from a booming brewery sat on top of it. But it began to buckle, and two guys jammed a log between the now-concave roof and the floor. They deemed the repair a success and recommenced loading the beer.

On the road, the driver opened up a case and passed around cervezas – including one to me. The fresh brew, soft sunlight and mountain air set the right tone. The driver, beer in hand, expertly picked his way over the first set of switchbacks, but the easy ambience was about to be shattered. The bus jounced and rocked on the rutted mountain track and it was too late for anyone to react when the log began to loosen. It crashed rudely on the head of a small child, splitting his scalp wide open.

The poor youngster wailed and his mother sobbed in panic. The driver hit the brakes and somebody tore a shirt into strips for a tourniquet. As near as anyone could tell, the impact had not broken his tiny skull. An older man flagged down a car heading back to town so the mother and child could get back to find a doctor. The log-rigging team re-did their work in dour quiet and the driver threw the bus into gear.

The ride ended in the hamlet of Pueblo Nuevo, the local bartender waddling out to greet the bus. He beamed at the beer shipment. I asked him about the commune and he told me it lay ahead three miles through the jungle. For a fistful of pesos, he let me store my bike in the back of his tavern. Still somewhat drunk, I trekked through the jungle as the sun dipped toward the horizon. I stuck to a straight trail until I saw the back of a tall man with red hair.

"Hey there!" I called out.

"Oh, hi. Who are you?"

"I came from Bogotá. I heard this place was open for people who wanted to work for food."

"Yeah, that's fine. It's just about dinnertime anyway. I was just finishing off here in the field. Come on, there's always enough for one more."

The man's name was Ned. On the way through the fields, he told me he was originally from Ireland and had come to Colombia seven years before, following a long stay in India. Ned and some others tilled a plot of land purchased from the Colombian government. They also raised cattle and bartered with farmers in the area. The Pueblo Nuevo settlement had ties to a bigger commune in another part of the country. Members travelled between the two places when they wanted a change of pace. The smaller commune now totalled three adults and bunches of children, many whose parents were said to live at the main Atlantis location. Until the previous week, Ned had been at the larger farm. With a mischievous smirk, he explained that his arrival had caused some problems.

"For two months it was just Mary and this other fellow, Alec, permanently here in Atlantis. Those two had been having sex until I got here. You see, part of what we do in Atlantis is to stir things up, being as direct about things as we possibly can. I told Alec I'd be taking over fucking Mary unless he had a plan to do something about it. Apparently he didn't."

A footpath appeared out of the yucca field, which guided us to a house. Kids were running all over the dwelling and a woman dished out plates of vegetable mash.

"We've got one more for dinner, Mary! This lad's from Canada and he's hungry. Dish him up a plate and we'll put him to work tomorrow," Ned shouted.

Mary obliged and, as the rest of us gobbled down a dinner of rice and vegetables, a stooped, bedraggled-looking man shambled in from the fields.

"Alec! You're late, man. You're not still pissed about the arrangement between me and Mary, are you?"

Mary dropped her eyes to the table. Alec said, "Oh, leave me alone."

"C'mon Alec, you know we like to get stuff out in the open here – get it off your chest man!"

"I just want to have my dinner in peace."

Alec was older than Ned by at least ten years, balding and wall-eyed. He exuded an oppressed energy, cowed by Ned. Mary, dark haired and attractive, was in her early 40s, between the two men in age and plainly the object of strife. Ned's red hair and beard matched his flaming temperament – lean, strong and very much enjoying his position as the one getting laid as well as chief tormentor. I found out later Ned had shelled out the cash for the Atlantis plot of land. By the conventions of the commune, that wasn't supposed to mean anything hierarchically, but Ned was definitely king of the castle.

Ned thrust a machete into my hands before I had wiped the sleep from my eyes the next morning. We spent two hours before breakfast cutting back underbrush. It was then I began to rethink the so-called sex farm idea. I had been warned about hard work on the commune, and hacking foliage at 6:00 AM made me feel every inch the migrant field worker I had become. In a more idiotic vein, the only sex going on apparently had to do with a lopsided competition between two men, and a woman in control of who got some. Mary later told me the only reason she had been sleeping with Alec was because he agreed to get up and start the kitchen fire every morning. The now-celibate Alec kept up with stove-lighting duties and Ned mentioned that to him every chance he got.

"Hey Alec, starting the fire are you? That's a good lad. I started a fire of my own last night, you know?" Or, "Alec, thanks for the fire this morning. It got Mary pretty hot!"

I couldn't tell whether Alec maintained the fire in hopes of regaining his 'in' status or if he'd resigned himself to martyrdom. Either way, this looked like a drag. Other than having just arrived, the only thing keeping me from taking off was the fact there was nowhere to spend money in Atlantis.

With no pressing reason to move on, I decided to stay. It was a decision I regretted often. One morning after milking the cows, Ned, his 14-year-old son and I hiked to Pueblo Nuevo to trade jugs of home-made wine. We'd sampled some a couple of nights before – it tasted like sugary citrus and packed a punch. The three of us carried two containers apiece, and I hoped the bartering would not drastically affect the home supply.

The discovery that we were swapping the wine for enormous sacks of potatoes was upsetting. Ned and I drank a beer and chatted with the bartender before doing any heavylifting. I could see my bike still sat in the backroom, apparently untouched. Ned refused my overtures to hang out for more beer – he wanted get back for breakfast. Heaving the sack onto my back, I walked behind the two others. The damned thing must have weighed 50 pounds. Ned's looked heavier still, and his son's couldn't have been much lighter than mine, but they quickly outpaced me and within ten minutes of leaving town I was lost.

Every step took me deeper into the woods, and the bag of potatoes felt heavier the more lost I became. The slight beer buzz had dissipated and left a sour feeling in my empty stomach, adding to my irritability. I tramped through bushes and threaded my way around massive trees in the thickets, swearing out loud. Hacking aimlessly about for more than an hour, I began to wonder if this was an initiation ritual – get the newbie good and lost in the bush and leave him there. Whatever the case, I began to harbour evil thoughts toward Ned. But I knew that attacking him with voodoo telepathy wouldn't help – figuring out the topography of the farm would. The property sprawled in all directions, some of it having been allowed to revert to jungle – a thing for which I had to credit the Atlantis people. With its constant plume of smoke, the farmhouse shouldn't have been hard to locate, but there was so much jungle in my face I couldn't tell whether I was close or miles away.

Another potato-lugging hour of futility dragged past. Then I saw cows. They grazed on a narrow, dung-covered track. I couldn't be far from the commune if they were Atlantis cows. All I had to do was squeeze past them and walk up the trail.

Impenetrable jungle grew on either side of the path, and the cattle, lined up single file, were impassable. I shouted at the animals and they moved ahead – for five feet. I yelled at them again and they moved five more feet. An almighty scream shot the procession ahead eight feet. This went on for two hours. With my back near buckling under the weight of the potatoes, I began to cry.

Tossing the sack aside in disgust, I cocked my head skyward and released a deluge of yowls and curses that rang throughout the jungle. The cows grazed placidly. I sat in the mud, despairing of seeing breakfast or any other meal that day. I wondered how long it would be before I dug into the bag of potatoes. Driven by hunger and fury at the cows, I sprang up and hurled another sustained barrage of screams. No more than a foot from the nearest cow, I harangued and yelled until the herd worked its way a magnificent 30 feet ahead. But, of course, when I stopped yelling, they stopped moving. Raw-voiced and panting, a terrible thought occurred: I had pushed the herd ahead but forgot the potatoes. I stood, shaking, four feet behind the rearmost cow. I could see the sack where I had left it at the side of the path.

I thought I'd have a nervous breakdown if the cattle reclaimed the muddy rut when I went back for it. I swore at the bovines, warning them not to follow me as I stumbled back to retrieve the spuds. The cows munched leaves, and made no move to retake the space. Now, with the sack on my back, I resumed yelling for 15 more excruciating minutes before the trail hit a stream. Ned and Mary had taken me to a swimming hole three days earlier and I hoped this was the same creek.

I walked in the river and water splashed over the rubber boots Ned had lent me. The thrill of losing the herd more than compen-sated for the backbreaking burden. Ten minutes later I caught a whiff of smoke that I hoped came from the farmhouse. Pushing along the stream with renewed vigour, I took a false step. The gravel bed gave way to a deep pool and I was up to my neck, but held the potatoes over my head.

Two hundred feet down, the slow-moving creek became shallow-er, coursing through a familiar-looking field. I remembered cutting my finger with a machete there two days before. I had tried to stanch the bleeding while continuing to clear brush. Ned saw the blood and sent me back to house, just a short hike from that spot. Now I stepped out of the stream and looked toward a clump of trees on a hill. The sky was grey that day as it often was, making it more difficult to spot the column of smoke. I found it after staring for a minute, and strode up the footpath. Dumping the sack on the kitchen floor, I told Mary that I wanted my breakfast.

"Well, fuck man," she said, "that's snotty of you, don't you think?"

I recounted the tale of cows, creeks and potatoes and she laughed from deep inside.

"Holy shit, we've had some sad cases of lost travellers up this way, but nothin' so silly as your adventure! Ha ha! We'll have you peeling those spuds for dinner tonight so you can go full circle with 'em!"

I gulped down some yucca and rice. I wasn't sure exactly when I'd leave Atlantis – but soon. That night I heard Ned and Mary having sex in the next room and then Ned telling Mary he was going to kick her in the face. At breakfast, I told them I'd be going the following morning. Mary smiled weakly, handed me a thick poncho and a wide sombrero and told me to pick coffee beans. She said that she knew I must have overheard the two of them the night before and tried to tell me that, according to Atlantis doctrine, she deserved what Ned was serving up. I told her that was her business and headed out for the coffee bushes.

Picking coffee was a worthwhile task for my last day on the farm. I chuckled as I gathered the wild beans from a certain hillside; of all the mental images of Colombia I'd collected before going there, picking coffee in the mountains was the most poignant. I still didn't know much about Colombia or its people, but spending a day acting out a Western cliché of the Colombian way of life set me momentarily at peace. I made a productive day of it and handed over the beans late that afternoon.

Taking pains the next morning to keep the trail that connected Atlantis with Pueblo Nuevo, the weird little commune all of a sudden impressed me as not so strange. I'd never worked harder in my life. The early hours in the field, milking cows, even picking up piles of shit with my bare hands for fertilizer were probably the same as the days of a billion other people. My bones ached and my hands still bled as I trudged along the path. The oddness of the whole journey started to fade, and I began to doubt whether the experiences I had once thought of as unique were in fact so isolated. The bar in Pueblo

Nuevo peeked through tufts of trees as I got closer to town, and I wondered, in spite of all I'd seen, if any experience could be completely original. I couldn't say.

Unable to make sense of it all, I envisioned an unsettling return to Vancouver. I would enjoy a warm reunion with my family, but before long, I would re-join my intimate pack of undesirables to drown in an ocean of liquor, years from a dry shore. The allure of familiarity was powerful. So was the unconscious desire to quell years-old anger and fear in the most convenient way. Trying to justify excessive boozing would be easier than lending a hand to any of the hundreds of desperate, worthy causes I'd encountered in the previous months. But the shelter of my favourite liquor store was a long way away; there were still thousands of highway miles ahead and lots could change before the last crossroads. A flicker of excitement energized me as I fitted the new tire onto my front wheel. Heart throbbing, I felt the hope of finding a meaningful link to the rest of the world. I hooked on my saddlebags and geared up for the next bend in the road.

~

Vancouver's baser haunts retained their lurid appeal and utility-grade beer. The Niagara, the Brickyard, the Cambie, the Pig and Whistle – even that alleyway den of rough Chinese food, the Green Door – lent shelter from the rushing lifeblood of city. Downtown was a rostrum of action, offering these few oases to marginal figures. The city funnelled slick-headed men in designer business suits off the street and into skyscrapers, men who rose up thirty stories, standing in elevators next to women in skirts and makeup who chewed gum to mask an odour of cigarettes. Outside the glass towers, traffic motored along the grid. Silkscreen reproductions of Toulouse Lautrec's designs sagged in the rain, hooked to rows of lampposts and announcing a coming display of the painter's work at the art gallery. Beggars took up customary positions on Granville Street and cash registers rang all day at buck-a-slice pizza joints. Toward the east side, at Main and Hastings, the open drug market never stopped and spent needles on the sidewalk exposed a rut of misery. Downtown supplied these sights, but bore the faded allure of a once-thrilling radio hit, now reduced to rote recital. The two-dollar-a-mug specials served at low-rent watering holes made all the difference.

I had made the inevitable return to scraping by as a bicycle messenger and to near-perpetual drunkenness. For a little over a year, I shared a house with a barbarous woman who viewed my penchant for draining oceanic quantities of liquor as an opportunity to get laid. A few times it worked for her. Finally scrambling to get away from this woman, I found a groovy little hovel in an ancient building in Vancouver's Gastown district. The place straddled skid row and the brick-path tourist area; occasionally, I saw disoriented German or Japanese travellers stumble in horror across a drug addict jamming a needle into a vein. The beauty of the apartment consisted not in the shared bathroom arrangement or its splintered hardwood floors, but in its proximity to the bars mentioned above. The Brickyard sat a mere block from my pad. The owners allowed couriers to wheel in their bikes, smoke with impunity despite a city-wide ban, and even tossed in the odd, free pitcher of beer. Alcoholism reigned supreme, but wanderlust lingered. In the summer of 1998 I headed south to spend a month hitchhiking and riding freight trains. The boxcar ride across Salt Lake, the police welcoming committee in the freight-yard outside of Phoenix, and the freak who stripped once I'd hopped into his car in Tennessee and drove naked to North Carolina, are stories for another time. But that refresher on the American backroads was enough to compel me to recalibrate my sights: across two oceans, to India.

Fuzzy impressions of Buddhist culture in the Himalayas along with the challenge of breaching the border into isolated Bhutan coloured my itinerary planning. Not that even the most imprecise outline of that trip existed; I hadn't so much as purchased a Lonely Planet travel guide. A friend of mine who had spent time in India told me to prepare for a boisterous and appalling tour. But the warnings of noxious filth, cauterizing heat and chasms of human suffering failed to impress; it would approximate a sort of far eastern stretch of South America. No worries. Besides, India ranked as one of the best places to travel on the cheap; accumulating walkabout cash without pulling back from my customary debauchery would be a snap. That formula proved simple to execute, which came as a relief because I had attained a new bottom: daily boozing. The power to stay out of the pub had evaporated; whether preparing for a scheduled spree or finishing a day of work, every single afternoon concluded in a bar. Even in Colombia, I had found myself periodically having to stop. Quotidian consumption continued until April 4, 1999. Only two months from taking off for New Delhi, I embarked on the fuck-up that nearly ended my life, but ultimately saved it. As deep down the abyss as my drinking had pulled me, I could not have foreseen the vicious hand of crack cocaine.

Drug dealers in the Gastown apartment building did a vigorous trade in Ecstasy, MDA and LSD, and occasionally I'd bang on one of their doors in a booze-induced coma at three in the morning demanding acid or X. Even in such a wasted stupor, I steadfastly refused coke – either rock or powder – which was also easily obtained in that neighbourhood. Sporadic experiences with the stuff as a very young man had demonstrated its annihilative power. But on the Easter Long Weekend of 1999, I sucked back so much whiskey that all inhibitions became void. I had begun the four-day holiday in the company of an old drinking buddy, and wound my way out to Surrey, one of Vancouver's most repellent, suburban dung holes. Two days of sloshing through hundreds of dollars' worth of liquor almost put me to sleep, but my companion and I decided to obtain some pep-pills. We staggered through a neighbourhood I'd never seen before and found ourselves sitting in Phil's kitchen. Phil laughed skittishly when we announced that we wanted to buy drugs. He didn't have any, but could get some. From what I can remember, Phil stood at about medium height with an atrophied frame and sallow, pitted complexion. This cadaver of a man made a call and 20 minutes later a mitt-full of crack sat on Phil's table.

I had paid for the rocks and protested that they be chopped into proper lines of coke – I may be breaking my 'no coke' rule, but damned if I was going to smoke crack like a common street addict. I had standards. Phil's roommate and my drinking buddy bitched that snorting rails amounted to a waste of quality crack. I relented, fired up a pipe, and two days later, I had blown 4,000 dollars. A whole year of savings and a trip to India were gone. The delirious combustion of the initial blast immediately sped on to a hideous finality; depression now scraped the depths of a suicidal hell. It was dawn and I tried to find the Alex Fraser Bridge so I could throw myself off of it. Vibrating with the worst of intentions, I flagged down a cab. Surely the driver would know where the bridge was. The man at the wheel asked where I wanted to go. I told him downtown. Maybe things weren't as bad as I thought; there were plenty of bridges downtown if I changed my mind. Back at my apartment, I got the first look at a mirror in four days. The reflection shot back a deranged look. Crack tar blackened my lips and teeth, bloodshot eyes sank into rawboned sockets and my hair was knotted. I hadn't showered after work on Thursday and still wore the same bike courier gear four days later. The stench of rancid sweat mixed with stale booze and two days' worth of crack forged the rank smell of death.

Forty-five minutes of scrubbing removed most of the crack stains from my mouth, but I had gone insane. Needing either to die or to re-cover the money I had squandered, speculation over whether I might successfully rob a bank rampaged through my brain. Hours later, a measure of lucidity returned. Destitute of any other ideas, I called my Mom. She drove over to my apartment and talked with me for a couple of hours, listening to what I had done. My Mom suggested I look into a Twelve-Step recovery plan. Seeing no other option, I attended a meeting that night, and every night after that for months.

Recovery rooms are terrifying places for the newly-minted sober alcoholic. Smirking know-it-alls spouting bad advice, other arrivals in equally brutal shape and a handful of skilled old-timers comprise a typical gathering of recovering drunks. The program recommends: 1) Obtaining a sponsor; 2) Attending 90 meetings in 90 days; 3) Becoming familiar with Twelve-Step literature; and, 4) Not drinking. I worked those basics hard, and I hung around with other newcomers; having similar problems and a common goal often makes for reliable allies.

At the time all this unravelled, I was enrolled in some general arts courses at a community college. Part of my plan for permanent sobriety involved hanging in and completing those classes. Cramming relentlessly for finals delivered the desired result; the grades were high enough that my university of choice admitted me. Still, the transition proved an agonizing one. The leap to university from college so early in recovery established itself as all but impossible to make. Times gone by remained deathly close up. Mediocre grades poured in from a full course load, and by October, I regarded it as certain that the task was insurmountable. The apparitions of failure, so familiar, bore down with suicidal virulence. Alone in my Gastown apartment, just out of a shower, naked and dripping wet, I dropped to the floor and wept. Twelve-Step wisdom holds that "alcohol was but a symptom" of spiritual deficiency; the full weight of a life lived in fear and shame exposed itself at that moment and I could not endure it. My previous method of living had proven untenable and, apparently, my vision of the future amounted to nothing better. Impassioned in the gravest sense, I trained a blurred gaze to the cracked ceiling and begged whatever power to intercede before the minute hand completed another turn.

Sometimes spiritual guardians have bloody hands. In the instant of harshest despair, a voice called my name from the street. My apartment had never been wired with an intercom and shouting from below served as the primary means of communication. I dare not describe the guy who yelled out; his appearance, mode of dress and vocal affectations must remain untold – I won't even assign him a pseudonym. All I can say is that, prior to his retreat from underworld activities and subsequent time in recovery, he had been into some bad shit. Gangster shit. But he saved my life. I was headed for dire, irreversible consequences had he not showed up when he did. Entering the apartment and seeing my condition, he told me to get it together; recovery meetings waited. The guy watched out for me in the weeks that passed. The two of us attended endless Twelve-Step meetings, we walked from one coffee shop to another and kept company with other ex-drunks, and the routine forced my thoughts out of their grim crannies. Slowly, university became less torturous: Descartes' "Meditations," the Big Bang theory and French grammar assumed degrees of manageability. The signposts of the future, for the first time, took on lustre rather than gloom.

It came as a relief that sober life still moved in offbeat directions. The flight to India that I had not long before traded for an evening of crack piping became a reality. So did a brilliant August of thumbing rides across Canada, as did another summer of jumping freight trains in the US. University led to journalism school and my first creditable job. Crisscrossing the frozen wastes of Northern Saskatchewan as a radio reporter and then plying my trade in the mountains of Southeastern British Columbia ultimately steered me into an ill-fated clash with the Supreme Court of Canada. Since then, wedding bells and hearings with American immigration officials have spirited me to the bayous of Louisiana. But the fulcrum necessary to lever away the death stones that almost weighed down soul and body could be found only through riding the road. Recovery programs emphasize the fact that "jails, institutions and death" await drunks who do not clean up; most who attempt the Twelve Steps stumble along the way.

Fortune has accompanied my own road to recovery, and I attribute much of this success to having seen what lies at the far end of the highway. Too often in recovery people return to drink because it serves as a stopgap for unfulfilled desire. My libidinous mania for travel found gratification, and on April 4, 1999 that satisfaction intersected with temperance.

An ancient Latin maxim says "solvitur ambulando" – it is solved by walking. Yes. Hit the road, blaze until your spirit can bear no more.

PHOTOGRAPHS

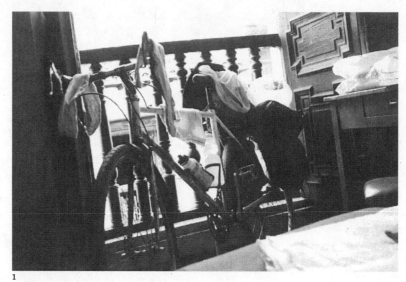

1 The bike that always broke down.
2 Tenting on Mexico's west coast.

1

2

3

1   A dip at a hot spring in Costa Rica.
2   Kitty cat rescue in Managua.
3   Downtown ghost town, Managua.

1   Hughes and a drinking buddy having a few primers at the Platypus.

2   Tyin' one on in Bogotá.

1   Hughes impersonating Huck Finn, Ecuador.
2   Huaorani hosts.

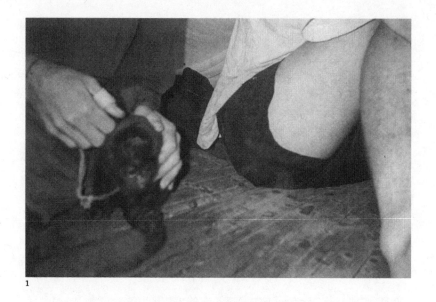

1 Dinner.
2 Gearing up to sail the Amazon.

1

2

1 Cramped quarters heading downriver.
2 Amazon slum.

Farther downriver.

COLOPHON

Typeset in Minion Pro. Manufactured in the Spring of 2012 by BookThug.
Distributed in the U S A by Small Press Distribution: www.spdbooks.org
Distributed in Canada by the Literary Press Group: www.lpg.ca
Shop on-line at www.bookthug.ca

BOOK
PRODUCTION
WAR ECONOMY
STANDARD

Type+Design: www.beautifuloutlaw.com